THE CRAFTY POET

Also by Diane Lockward

Temptation by Water
What Feeds Us
Eve's Red Dress
Greatest Hits: 1997-2010 (chapbook)
Against Perfection (chapbook)

The Crafty Poet

A Portable Workshop

by

Diane Lockward

WIND PUBLICATIONS
2013

International Standard Book Number 978-1-936138-62-3
Library of Congress Control Number 2013945348

First edition

The author thanks the wonderful poets who contributed their work to this book. She also thanks the many publishers who generously made their poems available to her. Finally, she thanks the subscribers to her monthly Poetry Newsletter who gave her a reason to write this book and who contributed sample poems.

Contents

III. Sound

IV. Voice

V. Imagery / Figurative Language

VI. Going Deep / Adding Layers

VII. Syntax

VIII. Line / Stanza

IX. Revision

X. Writer's Block / Recycling

List of Authors

Introduction

This book evolved out of a monthly newsletter I started in 2010. Simply called the "Poetry Newsletter" and sent by email, it initially went to about 100 subscribers, most of whom I'd invited. Each month, as word spread, I picked up new subscribers and soon had to move to a mailing service that could accommodate the larger number. The early newsletters included a recommendation for a book on craft or the writing life, a video, some links, and a model poem with a prompt based on the poem.

I then added another feature that quickly became one of the most popular: a Craft Tip solicited from an established poet. These tips covered a wide range of topics from generating ideas to revision. My subscribers sometimes wrote and said that between the craft tip, the model poem, and the prompt, they'd managed to write a new poem. Sometimes they said they'd written a poem after a long dry spell. Sometimes they sent me their poems, and it became clear that the newsletter was stimulating some very fine work.

By the time I hit the two-year mark, I had accumulated quite a bit of material, and it occurred to me that I might put it all together into a book for aspiring and practicing poets. The book I had in mind would include the craft tips, model poems, and prompts. But I thought it might also be instructive to include some pieces from the poetry blog I've kept since 2007. An occasional feature at *Blogalicious* is called "The Poet on the Poem." This feature includes one contemporary poem followed by a discussion with the poet. My method has been to find an intriguing poem, then contact the poet and ask if he or she would be willing to engage with me in a Question & Answer session. Every poet I asked accepted my invitation. My questions, five or six for each poem, are based on a close reading of the poem and focus on issues of craft. The responses are enormously illuminating and should dispel any idea that poems happen by pure inspiration. They come from the hard work of learning and practicing the craft of poetry.

There's a philosophy behind this book. I believe that courses and workshops are great. I've taken lots of them. As a poet who came late to the party and wasn't able to do an MFA, local courses and summer workshops were where I acquired my poetry education. I supplemented that work with books and more books. Because I believe in the autodidactic method of learning, I have attempted to construct a book that can be used independently, as well as in a group or in a classroom. It is my hope that this book will provide poets and poetry students with a good deal of education and inspiration.

The prompts I used in the newsletter and which I offer here came out of my belief that our very best teachers are the poems we read. Thus, each of the prompts begins with a poem. By studying the individual poem closely and noticing its moves, we can expand our repertoire of skills. We can then take what we've learned and put it to work in our own new poem. While such a poem might begin with imitation, through subsequent multiple revisions, it takes on its own identity and ends up bearing little resemblance to the model poem. Some of these prompts will result in poems that are *keepers*, while others will not. Regardless of the outcome, you will have practiced and honed techniques that will serve you well in future poems.

This book is organized by poetic concept into ten main sections. Other concepts not included in the Table of Contents are covered significantly in the prompts and in "The Poet on the Poem" Q&As. So you can expect to pick up some pointers on punctuation, anaphora, apostrophe, and the like. Each of the ten sections begins with a quotation intended to stimulate thought and discussion. Each section then includes two or three

Craft Tips. Each tip is followed by a model poem and prompt. Each prompt is followed by two sample poems solicited from the subscribers to my Poetry Newsletter. The last Craft Tip in each section is followed by one of "The Poet on the Poem" Q&As. I have attempted to place these logically, but you will find some overlapping of concepts and techniques. Each section ends with a Bonus Prompt. Bonus Prompts are offered without model poems and are in the nature of strategies that can be used repeatedly, thus making the day with nothing to say a thing of the past.

The poets included in this book bring contemporary voices from across the US and represent a variety of styles. A total of fifty-six poets contributed the Craft Tips, the poems in "The Poet on the Poem" Q&As, and the model poems for the prompts. These fifty-six poets include thirteen current or former state poets laureate. An additional forty-five poets contributed the fifty-four sample poems written to the prompts, most of these poems published here for the first time. These sample poems are intended to illustrate the possibilities the prompts might lead to. Some of them adhere closely to the prompts while others stray freely. When used in a group or classroom, they should generate some lively discussions and debates.

The Crafty Poet assumes a fairly knowledgeable reader. It is not intended to be a beginner's book. You will not find definitions provided for terms used. Nor will you find exercises designed to get you to practice skills such as writing metaphors. However, this is not said to discourage anyone from proceeding further. If you find a term used that you are not familiar with, simply put down this book and go to another for a definition. Then come back here.

Diane Lockward

I. Generating Material / Using Time

Those who have caused us early pain and loneliness,
the sources of our art:
should we detest them or kiss their feet?

—Wesley McNair

Craft Tip #1: Where Inspiration Waits for You

—Bruce Dethlefsen

Identify your best sources of inspiration. Return to them when needed. For me, it's the Three R's: Reading, Regarding, and Remembering.

When I read a poem that knocks me out, I try to figure out how the poet did that to me and where can I go with this. It's as if the poet built a swimming pool of ideas. Do I want to jump into the deep end or the shallow end, stick my toe in from the ladder, or soar from the diving board? After reading such a poem, consider the following:

1. Is there an image that grabs you? If so, try to imitate it in a new poem.

2. Is there something about the syntax, some unusual sentence structure that you might try your hand at?

Regarding and observing is my second best source of inspiration. When I was in college, I sat at the bus terminal and watched people come and go. Good poets belong in a witness protection program. Make the following practices part of your routine:

1. Never leave home without a small notebook.

2. As you quietly observe, take some notes. If you don't, those observations might be gone by the time you get home.

Remembering is my third best source of inspiration. I've constructed a big house with some sixty rooms for me to visit any time I want. I choose a room and look around, say room thirteen, where I see myself at the sock hop, in my white socks, hoping to work up the courage to ask some girl to dance. On any given day, you can begin this way:

1. Make a list of important events from a particular year or part of a year, for example, the summer of '66.

2. Choose one and freewrite about it. See where it takes you.

Poem and Prompt

Flying

I have a flying dream,
have since I was a kid.
In it, I remember suddenly
how to fly, something
for some reason I've forgotten;
by getting to a certain place
in my mind, I'm able simply to rise.
I go up only about sixty or seventy feet,
but that's high enough to look down on
my house, the one I grew up in,
in Tuscola, look down on it
and the trees of the neighborhood;
it's high enough to watch my father
from above as he leaves for work,
to see my mother as she gathers grapes
from the backyard arbor,
to see my sister in her pretty dress,
pulling all her friends in our wagon
down the long, new sidewalks,
to see our many dogs over the years—
high enough to see the blur of childhood,
to put my quiet shadow over all of us
early on. In the dream it's a summer's day
and I might sometimes also
be the one looking up, squinting hard
and seeing way high above
birds moving, black spots against the blue.

—Philip F. Deaver

Deaver takes a conventional approach to the poem of imagination, that is, he begins with a dream. This allows him to make the impossible possible, to make us suspend our disbelief. He goes back in time to childhood and places himself in the sky. From there he looks down on his childhood home and gives us a catalog of things he sees. He uses first person, and, although he's writing about past experience, he uses present tense. Thus, the scene is dynamic, and we feel as if we are witnessing it. Let's give this way of approaching memory a try.

Put yourself into a dream-like state and go back to an earlier time. You might return to your old house, but you could also return to school or summer camp or the hospital. Now recall images and memories. (Feel free to invent.) Quickly write them down. Select the best ones and the ones that work together. Where could you be as you observe the scene—in a tree, on the ceiling, on the roof? What imaginative way could get you there?

Now do a 10-minute timed draft using the images and memories.

Notice how Deaver brings some complication into his poem by introducing the *shadow* towards the end, the shadow he cast over his family. Makes me wonder. But I'm glad that he doesn't explain this. Leave some mystery in your poem, too. Avoid the temptation to explain or edit out what's mysterious.

Deaver uses free verse. Note his line breaks. Pay attention to your own.

In subsequent drafts, consider how your poem might change if you used past tense and third person.

Sample Poems

Mistaken

Only in the dead of night my mother,
lost to the seismic quake in her chest,
returns to my unbridled delight.

Not gone at all.
She wastes no time in preparing
chicken pot pie,
lasagna,
a big, thick steak.
From the head of the table, she pours wine.
In our gold-washed room, I crouch at her side,
press my face against her flushed cheek,
inhale her honeysuckle,
feel in her kiss the soft landing of a Monarch.

And my family, we—
all laughing and talking—reach
for seconds, for one more hunk
of honeyed bread from her hands.
Greedy, we demand more
and she hurries to the kitchen,

doesn't return. A cloud blinds us.
In the darkness, we keen like wolves.

And then I awake,
the aftershock
more shattering than the dream.

—Linda Simone

The Dream

A great soft arm
reaches down from the sky,

turned up for me to climb.
I dance in the palm,

shimmy my way up, heel
a little jig, and drop to curtsey

before two huge eyes,
open as a schoolhouse

airing itself out, its dusk echo
an invitation to the past. Yes,

I remember this. Tetherball,
hopscotch, my pet rock Sally.

When I lost her, I cried.
Same when I skinned my knee,

killed my favorite frog. See me
there—child of heartache

and tangled vines, tall forts
and trampolines—taming whole

universes with my star-tipped wand.
The seats of my swing set—

cushions on thrones.
What can I hope for now

that I couldn't imagine then?
I might stretch my own

great arm to memory, smudge
these fingertips with dream stuff,

and turn my palm up to everything
that wants to dance with me.

—Melissa Studdard

Craft Tip #2: Using Another Poet As Muse

—Cecilia Woloch

One strategy that's often helpful to me in the generative phase is to simply immerse myself in the work of a single poet whose language and music excite and, ideally, also mystify me a bit; I read and then I try to write my way into that language, that music, that sensibility—which is, of course, impossible. But the effort tends to lead me into a different place in my own sensibilities and relationship to language, and that takes me wherever it takes me.

Once I get going on something, I'm happy. Even if it doesn't result in any new poems, the exercise, alone, of trying on another poet's voice, seems worthwhile to me—a kind of cross-training and a way to experiment without being too self-conscious about it. And since I don't want to repeat myself—as Anne Carson has written, *I'll do anything to avoid boredom*—this exercise moves me away from saying and doing what I've already said and done.

To assure that my new poem is not too derivative, I read its lines backward—that is, in reverse order, from last line to first. This helps me to hear each line individually, and to hear how it's working as a unit, and also to hear if the overall music of the poem is really working. Sometimes this exercise has resulted in my re-ordering the sequence of lines in a poem or turning the whole poem upside down.

Poem and Prompt

More Lies

Sometimes I say I'm going to meet my sister at the café—
even though I have no sister—just because it's such
a beautiful thing to say. I've always thought so, ever since

I read a novel in which two sisters were constantly meeting
in cafés. Today, for example, I walked alone
on the wet sidewalk, wearing my rain boots, expecting

someone might ask where I was headed. I bought
a steno pad and a watch battery, the store windows
fogged up. Rain in April is a kind of promise, and it costs

nothing. I carried a bag of books to the café and ordered
tea. I like a place that's lit by lamps. I like a place
where you can hear people talk about small things,

like the difference between azure and cerulean,
and the price of tulips. It's going down. I watched
someone who could be my sister walk in, shaking the rain

from her hair. I thought, even now florists are filling
their coolers with tulips, five dollars a bundle. All over
the city there are sisters. Any one of them could be mine.

—Karin Gottshall

Have you ever had an imaginary friend or relative? Perhaps that person filled some emptiness or loneliness in your life. Or perhaps the invention satisfied some creative urge inside you.

For this prompt use the *palimpsest* method, that is, impose a new poem on top of the model poem. Place a piece of paper to the right or the left of the poem. Then begin at the beginning and go line by line, doing what the poet has done. Let the first stanza introduce a lie. Try to keep to the sentence structure used by Gottshall. Where she has a metaphor, you have one, too. Follow her pattern of enjambment from line to line and stanza to stanza.

In subsequent drafts, feel free to abandon whatever doesn't seem right. Let the poem go where it wants to go. Chances are that the poem you end up with will bear little, if any, resemblance to the original.

Sample Poems

Waiting for My Friend

Sometimes I say I'm going to meet my friend in the park—
even though I have no friend—just because I'd really
like to have a pal, a buddy, someone to listen when I talk

That sounds so nice—*my friend is waiting for me*—
the same as in the conversation I heard last week about
two friends who did everything together—talk, walk, shop

Today I carried a book and walked alone along the tree-lined street
stopped at a public bench—as though expecting someone
to meet me, looked at my watch to check the time

Anyone observing would think my friend were late
and I a patient person counting on his or her arrival
Someone might ask and I would say we were going to a party

for yet another friend—who was waiting for us at the door
of the restaurant, ready with a quick hug and cheery welcome
Then I watched someone who could be my friend get off the bus

looking around for the expected greeter and when she appeared
they walked off together keeping pace with each other's footsteps
as I pretended that the next person off the bus might be my friend.

—Ann DeVenezia

From a Lithuanian Courtyard

Today I am going to say I am Lithuanian—
though I have no Baltic blood at all—
because I want to know friendship like a bee,
because I want to have rain at my core.

Today I think I have always wanted to be
Lithuanian, to inflect with ease, palatize
my Ls like a Lithuanian, feel them soften
in my mouth—now resinous, now hard.

My language only knows one L, and allows
only one negative at a time. In Lithuanian,
I am not Lithuanian never. My history
branches back to everywhere, no accumulation

anywhere. But today I'm going to walk the streets
of Vilnius and wait for rain to fall in great drops
from a sudden sky, and get wet like a Lithuanian, briefly,
before stepping out of the road like a Lithuanian

into the shelter of a passageway to a courtyard.
At home there are no passageways and no courtyards,
only the great organized concourses of houses
and lawns, side streets and highways,

and the forested hills beyond scattered
with tumbling stone walls enclosing nothing.
I like the candor of a courtyard retreat,
its acknowledged need of an exit. For one day,

I am going to lie, say I am Lithuanian—
a bee who knows my friends' survival
depends on the dance of my language,
and on my setting out, and on my return.

—Lisken Van Pelt Dus

Craft Tip #3: Scratching

—Michelle Bitting

One of the greatest obstacles writers face in developing a strong creative practice, especially those of us raising children and holding jobs outside the home, can be carving out the time to actually set pen to paper, fingers to keyboard. As if striking generative gold, the excavation of scintillating syntax, language, and turns of thought and emotion weren't challenging enough.

During periods when life piles on unruly mounds of work and domestic duties, bereft of real writing time, I grow increasingly anxious and moody. I worry I will slip out of the creative zone I've worked so hard to tap—ideas will fade, metaphors atrophy—I'll wake up an exile from my own poetry country.

The good news is I know I'm not alone. And I know one of the greatest tools we possess is the ability *to scratch*, to jot something down on paper in the briefest, skinniest interstices of the busiest day, week, month, year. It's an old and obvious practice, but I believe it is essential to anyone interested in maintaining a true writerly life.

I remember reading that poet Mary Jo Bang would scribble random thoughts and observations walking or riding the train during her busy teaching week when that was all she could grab. Nuts and berries gathered into the basket of a pocket notebook that eventually might transform into a poetic fare as it marinated along in her unconscious.

The great choreographer Twyla Tharp devotes an entire chapter in her book, *The Creative Habit*, to the subject of "Scratching," suggesting *it's like clawing the side of a mountain to get a toehold, a grip, some sort of traction to keep moving upward and onward ... It's primal and very private.*

Julianna Baggott, a highly prolific writer, suggests a daily practice broken down into three parts that focus and make specific one's scratching routine:

1. Memory Exercise: Jot down three memories from the distant or immediate past. A sentence or two or even just a sensuously descriptive phrase.

2. Eavesdropping Exercise: Write down three things overheard during the day. Snippets you catch in line at the grocery store, from the radio, from someone blabbing too loud on his cell phone.

3. Image Exercise: Notice things. Gestures. Junk. Movement. Detritus. Smoke billowing up behind the supermarket bakery. The Psychedelic Anarchy sticker someone slapped on the top of the signal lamp at the crosswalk where you are standing.

When time finally permits, pick a few of the items from each category and use them to create something. Coax them gently without forcing it too hard, letting the thoughts and images bob and bounce, having faith magic may surface that resonates. Even if the sum of the parts doesn't converge into a *keeper* poem, you've done a little scratching to stay in the zone and keep up your writerly chops. There may be one item, one berry you've collected that spins you off into a wonderland of unexpected thought or investigation. Worse things could happen! You're in the groove and working. You are writing.

Poem and Prompt

The Interior Decorator Advises

The decorator said, you need something soft
like air.
Grass and stars
belong over there.
Hang the cost. Move the window.
Steeple and bell
constitute a view.
Extend the door.
By and by you will grow.
Embrace more.
Coarsen. Widen
Cold and sand
will find their welcome
like it or not.
In the back room where you retreat
maybe a cat or dog.
Children seem beyond the scope
of what you meant.
And probably not a loveseat.
Over here—with your ghosts
just the right puce. But not
too much. It's necessary
to blend. Anything else—
like ochre—will require
more fabric. Sackcloth or grosgrain.
Remember, whatever is left out
can't be seen.

—Robert Bense

Notice that Bense uses diction drawn from the world of interior decorating: *loveseat, puce, ochre, fabric, sackcloth, grosgrain.* But he also employs seemingly unrelated diction: *grass, stars, steeple, sand.* Strive for this kind of mixture with your own diction.

Notice, too, that the work of the interior decorator takes on a secondary meaning. It is not a house or a room that is being redesigned but the interior life of the *you,* the person being addressed. This might come into your poem naturally. If not, make it happen. Go for that kind of texture.

Now for your challenge. Write out this statement: "The _____ said, you need." Fill in the blank with the name of another kind of worker, e.g., a plumber, accountant, landscaper, cosmetologist, or painter.

Before you begin writing, brainstorm a list of words that might be used by your worker. If your worker is a plumber, you might list *wrenches, hot water heater, pipe, plunger.* Now pick up with your opening line and keep going, just freewriting at first. Pull in some of the words from your brainstorming list. Add some contrasting diction.

Sample Poems

The Conversation

A designer friend drops by,
goes to my mantle and moves
two vases—*They need to be close,*
need to be in conversation, she says,
and then to me, *I love to push you around.*

I wonder if my vases are happier,
wonder if I've deprived them,
wonder how my designer friend
knows so much about vases
and so little about me.

—Jeanie Greensfelder

Solving the puzzle

The cruciverbalist said I needed
a pencil, not an ink pen.
Solving my crossword with permanent
ink is arrogance, he said.
At first I listened.
Tried to write my life in pencil.
Timidly.
Was sure I could rub out everything
that didn't fit.
The pencil marks had
penetrated too deep.

I gained courage.
Acquired a certain bluster.
When it came to
finding solutions,
I applied what I knew:
audacity,
braggadocio,
chutzpah,
nerve,
insolence,
presumption,
pretentiousness,
smugness,
but it was only six across
and started with an H.
HUBRIS.

It took me forever,
but eventually I filled
the final squares. Did it with
a magic marker.
An intentional response to promote well-being,
five down:
AGAPE.

—Rose Mary Boehm

The Poet on the Poem: Bruce Guernsey

October

Today, they're cutting the corn,
the stalks dry and blowing, brown
and rattling, rattling
when you walk by
as if something were inside,
a deer, a coon, something
alive, someone maybe.
But today
they're cutting it down
as they do every October,
the combines on the back roads,
on the fields,
working all night, next day and next,
until the land is flat again
and we can see
some ranch house we forgot
a mile or so away.
Out here
the corn is a special mystery,
a haunted place
where children warned not to
want to play.
No wonder each September
before the harvest
some farm kid disappears,
losing himself in the tall acres,
tunneling under the sabers
rattling over his head,
vanishes for hours, for days.
Usually, they come back
or are found; once in a while,
they're not. That's why

slowing to a walk
somewhere out from home
and out of breath,
I always stop, sure I've heard
something in there,
something I woke jogging by,
one of those kids maybe
in the forest of corn,
hear him, the closer I get,
running away.

DL: I admire the way you use repetition in this poem. It slows the poem to a pace appropriate for a walk in the country. At the same time, it increases the tension as it holds us back when we want to move forward. Tell us about your use of this technique and what you hoped to achieve with it.

BG: There are indeed a lot of repetitions in the poem, but the ones that mattered to me when I was writing were patterns of sound more than whole words—the long vowels of the first sentence, for example: the *a* in *today* (used twice), *they*, and *maybe*, and the high-pitched, long *i* sounds of *dry*, *by*, *inside*, *alive*.

Such sound patterns are what always lead me forward in writing a poem although I am never fully conscious of them at the time. Thus, following my ear is not really a *technique* as such. It's far more intuitive than that. But those long vowels do add to the tension, especially the siren-sound of the *i*. These are the poet's background music that the movie-thriller uses so blatantly.

The repeated words do function rhetorically to slow the pace, but the tension really comes from those words being set against the frequency of high-pitched vowels. It's not the repetition of words alone that creates tension but how the easy pace of repetition works against the more alarming sound patterns, like hearing an ambulance in the distance on a calm summer night.

DL: The diction in this poem is the language of everyday speech. But certain word choices seem essential and strategic, e.g., *cutting, rattling, sabers, mystery, haunted, warned.* At what point in the writing of the poem did you consider word choice? Did these words appear in the first draft or subsequent drafts?

BG: October is the month of goblins and ghosts, so there's no doubt that I was trying to get some of that conventional language in there. But firstly and mostly, I was trying to describe what I heard. The dried corn does indeed rattle in the wind, and you'd swear there was something in it. I wanted to be visually accurate, too: the sharp-edged leaves do have a saber-like look to them which fit in nicely with the *rattling,* and with the *tunneling* as I began to imagine a sort of gauntlet scene with the child running under the drawn swords of corn. As so often happens, I simply got caught up in my own imaginings, and the world I was living in became the poem itself.

One thing I do remember in revising was the debate I had about the house we could see once the corn was cut. I originally wrote *farm house,* then later thought that *ranch house* more dramatically revealed the leveling of the harvest and, in a way, made it more likely that a child might seek the mystery of the vertical corn as compared to the flatness of such a home.

DL: I like the way the poem moves from peaceful to frightening. It takes several subtle turns. The child vanishing in the corn seems innocent enough. But then you say, *Usually, they come back / or are found...* That *Usually* is ominous. It made me think that sometimes a child comes to harm. Then there's another shift at the end. Tell us about that, how you arrived at that. Did you surprise yourself?

BG: Many of my students at Eastern Illinois University grew up on farms, and they told me about playing in the corn and sometimes getting lost in it. One even told me the story of a friend who did indeed never come back. The child simply disappeared. I certainly had that possible horror in the back of my mind when I started the poem.

Around the time I was working on this poem, my own father disappeared from the rural VA hospital he was in. He had Parkinson's disease and one day somehow got himself dressed and walked out the door of the ward he was in and vanished. We never found him despite the extraordinary searching that went on.

No doubt I brought my own ghosts to this seemingly innocent scene of the cornfield and harvest. So, in a way, I am not surprised the poem ended the way it did, though Freud would wonder why I had a child *running away* at the end rather than his father.

DL: You've lived in three distinctly different environments— New Jersey, New England, and now the Midwest. And I read in your bio that you've twice sailed around the world. You've referred to Nature as a *feast for the imagination*. What influence have place and change of place had on your work? On this poem?

BG: When I first moved to Illinois, the flatness of the prairie gave me the perspective I needed to write about my native stone walls and pine forests. The same stones and those dark woods also made me look at the open fields of the Midwest in a far different way than did those who grew up here. Thus, in my long runs on the open roads that square off the cornfields of east central Illinois, I might hear *something / alive, someone maybe*, while others might hear only the wind.

New soil and fresh water can be as good for us as for any root-bound plant.

DL: You were the editor of *Spoon River Poetry Review*. What effect has being the editor of a poetry journal had on your own poetry? Is that another kind of feast? Or do you risk losing your appetite?

BG: One can overeat, of course, but my stint as editor at *Spoon River* was quite a feast. I was fortunate to read some great poetry that I would never have come across otherwise, and then to have the opportunity to make that work known to others was simply wonderful. Nothing pleased me more during those years than to publish someone for the first time. I frequently called the poet to say I was taking the poem, and that was just a joy, a real privilege.

Bonus Prompt: The Fruitful Memory Poem

Directions:

1. Choose a fruit or vegetable for your poem. Look at it carefully from all angles.

2. Quickly describe how it looks. Consider color, size, and shape.

3. Describe the smell.

4. Describe how it feels.

5. Describe how it tastes.

6. Make a few similes, e.g., It looks like _____ It is as beautiful as _____ It is soft as _____ It is more yellow than _____.

7. What can you make with this fruit? Brainstorm a list of dishes.

8. Write a memory associated with your fruit. Don't have one? Make it up.

9. Now use all this material in a new poem. You may keep the above order or rearrange.

Revision Suggestions:

1. Do a Google search on your subject to find new information and snazzy diction. Import some of what you find into the draft.

2. Rewrite from the point of view of the fruit or vegetable.

II. Diction

The difference between the almost right word and the right word ... is the difference between the lightning bug and the lightning.

—Mark Twain

Craft Tip #4: Words with Muscle

—Pam Bernard

When crafting a poem, I am concerned most with how to sharpen the sense of enactment, which can create a conduit for the reader to more deeply enter the experience I wish to convey. A poem ought to change the reader's molecules in some fundamental way, but, in order to achieve this, we must provide language with muscle—verbs with edges, palpably visible nouns, as few adjectives as possible, and even fewer articles. It's not simply an issue of compression or diction, but the creation of a visceral experience on the page—right there, right then.

But how can we create words that mean more than the sum of their parts? Chiefly it is through valuing craft—by shaping and reshaping language towards enlarged meaning. Words become a breathing, palpable presence, a region of correspondence between reader and writer.

Poets ought not be far from their words. As different as these poets' works are in tone, style, and subject—Hopkins's word-drunk passion, Kunitz's spare elegance, or Glück's dark, intellectual interrogations—all embody enactment. The poem is not a relic of an emotional experience, but the experience itself.

Will you give your reader a piece of white paper with words on it, or the small, warm animal of your hand?

Poem and Prompt

Because I Never Learned the Names of Flowers

It is moonlight and white where
I slink away from my cat-quiet blue rubber truck
and motion myself to back it up to your ear.
I peel back the doors of the van and begin
to hushload into your sleep
the whole damn botanical cargo of Spring.

Sleeper, I whisk you
Trivia and Illium, Sweet Peristalsis, Flowering Delirium.

Sprigs of Purple Persiflage and Lovers' Leap, slips
of Hysteria stick in my hair. I gather clumps of Timex,
handfuls of Buttertongues, Belly buttons and Bluelets.

I come with Trailing Nebula, I come with Late-Blooming
Paradox, with Creeping Pyromania, Pink Apoplex,
and Climbing Solar Plexus,

whispering: Needlenose,
Juice Cup, Godstem, Nexus, Sex-us, Condominium.

—Rod Jellema

I admire the wordplay in this poem, the sexiness of it. The language is romantic, fanciful, and musical. Notice the made-up words like *cat-quiet* and *hushload*. And the beauty of the flower names. Real names, made-up ones, or silly ones, they are fun to say, to roll around in the mouth.

Notice the sound devices, e.g., the alliteration in *Buttertongues, Belly buttons and Bluelets*. And the rhyming of *Paradox, Apoplex, Plexus, Nexus, Sex-us*. Wouldn't it be lovely to be that Sleeper and have someone whispering all this into your ear as you nod off?

Choose a category, perhaps fruits, vegetables, birds, or fish. Or choose something within the category, e.g., apples, beans, or lettuces—something that has variety. Then create a bank of words with great sounds, some rhyming words, some near rhyming words. Let some of those words be nouns, some verbs, a few adjectives. Make up some of the words. Make your word choices delicious.

Imagine an auditor.

Then begin with *Because I never learned the names of* _____ .

Drawing from your word hoard, write a poem delivered very privately to your auditor.

In revision change your poem to make it uniquely yours.

35

Sample Poems

Radish

The radish malodorous culpable is.
    —Sylvester Feliney

White moon in fuchsia stocking,
Ishtar's brandish, amateurish cherry,
Kaddish ruby, garish tadpole,
fleshy radicchio-less dish.
What English can accomplish: ravish the ear,
shush the rational, *pshaw* the varnished,
astonish anguish with gibberish.
Oh, rakish garnish, ravish my tongue
with your gnashing kisses—grant
my childish wish to be special—
to relish as lush, ingest as delicious,
what only the famished can cherish.

                    —Susanna Rich

Love Apples

In one of our rarest moments of intimacy,
my mother confessed to me

her love for the tomato, how she used
to pick them straight off the vine,

tearing away the warm globes that were
basking only moments before,

then breaking into the soft, cartilaginous
walls of their chambers

to feel the surge of their seeds, the rasp
of acid on the back of her tongue.

She said tomatoes spread an ugly rash
on her cheeks, which was why

she'd given them up long ago. I stared
more closely at her face then,

clear and papery-white like mine, and
thought how good it would feel

to be rash, to let hunger briefly inflame
me. Skin like a crimson scar.

—Jeanne Wagner
published in *Alehouse*

Craft Tip #5: Finding the Right Words

—Diane Lockward

One of the qualities that distinguishes an outstanding poem from a merely competent one is language that sizzles, sings, and surprises. And yet too many of us settle for ordinary language when extraordinary language is available and free to everyone.

Consider the diction of John Donne in "A Valediction: Forbidding Mourning." The poet startles us by using mathematical language to describe two lovers: *If they be two they are two so / As stiff twin compasses are two; / Thy soul the fixed foot, makes no show / To move, but doth, if th' other do.* In another love poem, "The Good-Morrow," Donne pulls diction from the field of cartography: *Let sea-discoverers to new worlds have gone; / Let maps to other, worlds on worlds have shown; / Let us possess one world; each hath one, and is one.* Donne often fused together language from two seemingly unrelated fields. If you haven't tried this yet, why not?

Consider, too, the diction of Gerard Manley Hopkins in "Pied Beauty" where the speaker gives thanks for *dappled things— / For skies of couple-colour as a brinded cow; / For rose-moles all in stipple upon trout that swim* ... Such language is delicious in our mouths and a joy to speak aloud.

For a more contemporary voice, listen to Sharon Olds in "One Year" as the speaker describes a visit to her father's grave: *I saw the speedwell on the ground with its horns, / the coiled ferns, copper-beech blossoms, each / petal like that disc of matter which / swayed, on the last day, on his tongue. / Tamarack, Western hemlock, / manzanita, water birch / with its scored bark* ... Notice the precision of the language. No vague *tree* for this poet but rather the specific names of trees, each one of them adding more music, interest, and imagery to the poem. Olds, like her predecessors, never settles for easy language.

Nor should you settle for the first words that come to you; go in search of the best words. But where to find those best words? You might start with the catalogs, unordered and unwanted, that fill up your mailbox. Don't be so fast to toss them out. Some of them may contain new vocabulary for your poems. Hang on to that flower brochure, the Harry and David catalog, the circular full of ads for local restaurants.

A simple Google search will often lead you to specialized websites where you can find a feast of language. Let's say you're writing a poem about blueberries. Googling just might lead you to the website for the Gierke Blueberry Farm in Michigan and then to esoteric information about blueberries, some tasty recipes, and words like *cultivars, domesticated, antioxidant,* and these lovely names of different kinds of blueberries. *Rabbiteye, Primadonna, Sapphire,* and *Snowchaser.*

Wikipedia is a great online source for new diction. Let's say you're writing a poem about a frog. Take a piece of paper with you to the computer and search *Wikipedia* for "frog." As you read through relevant articles, jot down words such as *carnivorous, amphibian, proto-frog, vertebrate, glandular,* and *planktivorous.* Use some of those words in your poem.

Keep your eyes and ears open. And, of course, keep a notebook where you store words you've discovered in catalogs, articles, and books, as well as words you've heard on the street, on TV, in a speech. You never know when you might need those words. They might generate a new poem or they might reinvigorate a failed draft.

Poem and Prompt

The Foley Artist's Apprentice

I wanted to be one of his props, a thing
that made the sound of other things—an umbrella
      pushed open and closed: birds' wings.
      A coconut shell, one half
in each of his hands—galloping,
      galloping. I set up his microphone stands
and he made the crackle of fire
      with a ball of cellophane,
      poured salt on a tinfoil sheet for rain.
The sound of skin on skin—two pieces of paper he slid
      against each other. I wanted to be the words
on the paper. I wanted to be what I heard
in the mixing studio as I layered and looped
      his tracks. I play them back:
my body the strip of steel he shook for thunder,
      the feather he held to the spinning bike wheel
      for a hummingbird's hum, the fine-toothed comb
on which he plucked the crickets' song. The real
sound isn't always the best,
      he said, when I asked why not go outside
and record the wind—and when I held
      the microphone to my chest what it amplified was less
like a heartbeat than the one he made
      when he wrapped
the microphone in felt and gently tapped
      it against a bass drum, again and again.

—Caitlin Doyle

In order to fully appreciate this poem, you need to know that a Foley Artist is someone who uses everyday objects to mimic sound effects to enhance the action in a film. Such a person typically works in the movie industry.

How appropriate, then, that Doyle uses such wonderful sound effects in her poem about being an apprentice to a Foley Artist. The rhyme pattern is erratic, but the poem is loaded with rhyming devices. There is some end rhyme—*thing* and *wings*, *wheel* and *real*, *wrapped* and *tapped*. But there's also the internal rhyme of *tracks* and *back*, *chest* and *less*, *layered* and *play*. There's also repetition—*thing* and *things*, *skin on skin*, *again and again*. Lots of alliteration, assonance, and consonance. And notice, too, the use of anaphora in the opening and then repeated *I wanted to be*.

Let's do an odd job poem. Your first task is to choose an odd job for the subject of your poem. Some possibilities: ocularist, beer tester, worm picker, chimney sweeper, body farm caretaker, chicken sexer, shark tank cleaner, water-slide tester, chocolate taster, and fortune cookie writer. After choosing your odd job, do a Google search. As you find appropriate articles, jot down some relevant language. You want words that are special to this job and words that sound great.

Then decide what your relationship is to your worker. Are you the worker? The apprentice? A spouse? The child of?

Using first person, write your draft. Employ some of the specialized diction.

In later drafts, work on the musical effects of the poem, especially rhyming.

Finally, decide on the format of your poem. Do you want indented lines as Doyle has used? Stanzas? Long lines or short ones or alternating lengths?

Sample Poems

My Man, the Green Man

Pyrotechnicians, known as Green Men,
would wear costumes of leaves and mud,
to protect them from stray sparks and remain
hidden from the crowds at firework displays.

He covers himself in clay and branches,
hidden in what protects him best:
dusky blanket, shadow, damp armor
against spiteful sparks or just one
watcher's *hmph* of disenchantment.

The crowd will never see my fine
firework-starter as he runs from fuse
to fuse, lighting sulfurous snakes,
thrusting bright magic to the skies,
higher than any have climbed

(though he takes me there, he does).
When he and his mates part, they say,
Stay green—safe, invisible, fertile,
invincible, wreathed in rainforest mist,
one redolent color and scent.

When we met at the royal fireworks
he called celebration a force, *a bodyless*
idea, rather like faith, that only exists
when expressed. I fell right there,
catching the campfire light in his, yes,

green eyes, the light his leaves give back,
those leaves leaking magic, the leaves
beekeepers-who-have-touched-the-dead
wash with before returning to the hive.
Celebration, ever since, equals love.

See how he calms my bag-of-cats temper,
soothes my brittle humours, douses anger
with wit, so laughter melts me in a sodden
clump. He can charm cranky children,
extinguish frustrations, smother spats.

He causes all that sparking glory, yet
stays camouflaged, self-effacing, green
santa of smoke. Coming home to the dark
still room, he smells of spent campfire.
I hug the leafy cloak, and he pulls me in.

When I rest my hair in his moss,
I revel, remembering that rainstorm
when we could not have gotten wetter.
He saves one last pinwheel rocket
for me. We drench each other.

I worry, yes. He could be gone
in a flash. But he comes from a tall
line of treeherders, patient, wet
behind the ears, therefore humbly wise,
deserving every ooh and ahhhh.

Come, let's ignite joy, create it
from bow drill and tinderbox,
burn the combustibles, soak
stinging cinders in sap, douse
ourselves in constancy, in camouflage.

—Tina Kelley

The Snake Milker's Daughter

I stand outside the serpentarium window,
   watching his captive asps—
      mambas, copperheads, vipers—
         coiling and recoiling in the vivariums:
      they who are always long longer
   than wide, limbless enough to slither.
They greet him, as he slips through the door—
   tongues tasting his musk,
      the rattlers in chorus,
       a symphony of sizzles—
      my circumscribed glass buzzing its frame.
   He unhooks a screen cover.
The taipan sidles to the far corner. He is the fullest.
   He must come first. My father loops the head
      in the triangular pin stick, hoists him
         onto the metal podium,
      under the funnel suspended
   under a vial. He pinches the head,
winds the body around his arm. The fangs
   penetrate the rubber membrane stretched
      over the mouth of the vial.
        The drip of yellow venom.
      The cucumber smell of fear.
   The serums, the antivenins.
The hearts and the blood it will save.
      The hardest thing is granting him freedom.
        I play my flute—my *pungi*, my *been*. I play
         for my father. For Cleopatra and Eden.
        For the times my father was bitten.

                 —Susanna Rich

Craft Tip #6: Importing New Words

—Marilyn L. Taylor

Here's a strategy to help you shake up and rescue a draft that's stalled out. Go through your notebook and make a list of twelve favorite words. Favorite words can be words that you simply like the sound of, words that bring something vivid to mind, words that you find particularly expressive. They can be of any part of speech. Compound words, like *fat-cat* or *junk bonds*, are fine, too. Just no long phrases.

Then go into your folder of work you've given up on. Pull out one abandoned poem and rewrite it so that it includes every single one of those twelve words. Adjust for tense, number, and so on wherever necessary

You will be amazed at the transformation, and it will all be because of diction.

Poem and Prompt

Advice from a Caterpillar

Chew your way into a new world.
Munch leaves. Molt. Rest. Molt
again. Self-reinvention is everything.
Spin many nests. Cultivate stinging
bristles. Don't get sentimental
about your discarded skins. Grow
quickly. Develop a yen for nettles.
Alternate crumpling and climbing. Rely
on your antennae. Sequester poisons
in your body for use at a later date.
When threatened, emit foul odors
in self-defense. Behave cryptically
to confuse predators: change colors, spit,
or feign death. If all else fails, taste terrible.

—Amy Gerstler

Gerstler's poem of personification should be fun to work with. Choose some creature from the world of nature. Consider the rat, the hummingbird, the tuna, the pig.

Brainstorm a bunch of facts about the creature. Where does it live? What does it eat? What does it look like? What is it good for? What trouble does it cause?

Now ask yourself: If that creature could speak and give advice, what might the advice be? Imagine yourself as that creature. Then write your draft in the voice of your creature. Use some relevant, dynamic diction.

Notice the short imperative sentences. And the occasional long one. Try that.

Give your poem a title that guides the reader into the poem.

Sample Poems

Advice from a Bat

Hunt only at night. Fly erratically.
Defy even your own expectations.
Feed on beetles, moths, and mosquitoes,
whatever is small and annoying.
Cultivate the myths about you
until every predator fears your legend.
When hunting, be guided by a language
only you can hear. The same is true
when courting the one you love.
Clean fangs and fur nightly. Crawl
or climb to confuse the observant.
Retreat to a cave no one believes in.
Let the day and the world pass
while you sleep, and sleep upside down,
ready to wake and fall into flight.

—Michael T. Young
published in *Off the Coast*

The Siamese Cat's Blues

When Paul comes home, the dog barks,
his whimpers betraying his fear
that the old boy had been lost in a storm.

Don't spoil him, Slobber Face.
I don't. I take up my old complaints
mid-stream from the last time

that Paul and I separated. No hello
or rubbing against his woolly socks.
I lead him straight to my bowl

to show him the source
of my unhappiness.
Will he ever learn to fetch properly?

To get his attention, I'm forced
to hide behind chairs, to pounce
at his ankles, claws flying.

Why is he so incapable
of meeting my demands?
The stupid mutt barks

like a seal to remind Paul
that the world is filled with gulls
that need to be chased.

Off they head to the park, Paul's
obligations unmet. I watch from the window
as they choose mud and burrs over me.

If my blue eyes were flames,
those two would surely burn.

—Bob Bradshaw

49

The Poet on the Poem: Martha Silano

It's All Gravy

a gravy with little brown specks
a gravy from the juices in a pan

the pan you could have dumped in the sink
now a carnival of flavor waiting to be scraped

loosened with splashes of milk of water of wine
let it cook let it thicken let it be spooned or poured

over bird over bovine over swine
the gravy of the cosmos bubbling

beside the resting now lifted to the table
gravy like an ongoing conversation

Uncle Benny's pork-pie hat
a child's peculiar way of saying emergency

seamlessly   with sides of potato of carrot of corn
seamlessly   while each door handle sings its own song

while giant cicadas ricochet off cycads and jellyfish sting
a gravy like the ether they swore the planets swam through

luminiferous   millions of times less dense than air
ubiquitous   impossible to define a gravy like the God

Newton paid respect to when he argued
that to keep it all in balance to keep it from collapsing

to keep all the stars and planets from colliding
sometimes He had to intervene

a benevolent meddling like the hand
that stirs and stirs as the liquid steams

obvious and simple   everything and nothing
my gravy your gravy our gravy   the cosmological constant's

glutinous gravy   an iridescent and variably pulsing gravy
the gravy of implosion   a dying-that-births-duodenums gravy

gravy of doulas of dictionaries and of gold
the hand stirs   the liquid steams

and we heap the groaning platter with glistening
the celestial chef looking on as we lift our plates

lick them like a cat come back from a heavenly spin
because there is oxygen in our blood

because there is calcium in our bones
because all of us were cooked

in the gleaming Viking range
of the stars

DL: I am delighted by the leaps this poem takes. How did you negotiate the progression from kitchen to cosmos, from real gravy to metaphorical gravy?

MS: My leaping guide in this poem is Pablo Neruda, especially his odes. I have read some of Neruda's food odes so many times it's like I have a Neruda microchip inside me. *Gravy of doulas of dictionaries and of gold* could easily have been lifted directly from a Neruda poem—not the exact words but the trope. Also, I had been doing a lot of research: Simon Singh's *Big Bang*, a biography of Newton, a book about Aristotle and his ether concept. And I'd been kicking around for months this idea of writing a poem titled "It's All Gravy." I didn't know what the poem would be about, but I had to make good on a promise to myself to write a poem with that title. Once the lucky accident of the cosmos research and the gravy idea merged in my head, the poem, at least an early (and mediocre) draft of it, emerged quite easily.

DL: Tell us why you dispensed with punctuation and sentences in this poem. And at what point in your drafting was that decision made?

MS: As far as I can tell from pouring over early drafts of this poem, there was never any punctuation or sentences. Dispensing with punctuation and sentences wasn't a logical or rational choice, but an intuitive one. From the very first draft, it felt like the poem should be fragmented and punctuation-less. Looking back on my choice, perhaps it had something to do with the subject matter—where we come from. It seemed so huge, as if ordinary grammar and punctuation could not contain it. It was like the words had to be flying through ether, or mingling with the carbon of dead stars. How could I place a period in a poem that was communing with the stars that made us?

DL: In several stanzas, you use white space. What do you see as the function of those open spaces? How do you accommodate them when you're reading the poem aloud?

MS: The white space was an experiment. In the past when I have written poems without punctuation, one of the problems I continuously encountered (and why I have come back to loving punctuation) was how to create pauses without periods, commas, semi-colons, and dashes. Usually that would mean a line break, but I did not want *seamlessly* on its own line, and the same with *luminiferous* and *ubiquitous*. I just wanted them set off from the rest of the line, so I copied what many writers do—I hit the space bar a few times. When I read this poem, I pause between the white spaces about the same length of time as I do for a line break.

DL: I'm also intrigued by your strict use of two-line stanzas. The formality of the form seems at odds with the absence of punctuation and sentences and the use of white space. What made you choose the form?

MS: Many of my poems are written in couplets, whether or not they are punctuated or written in sentences. Very often early drafts are written without stanzas, or in three-line or four-line stanzas, but usually the poem does not start taking off until I put it into couplets. I am not sure why this is the case. I never wrote a poem in couplets until Linda Bierds pointed out that I had that option. She explained that certain poems might warrant the two-line stanza, for example, a poem with two opposing forces, one about two people, or one with an either/or situation. It turned out that just about all of my poems present dualities, couplet-worthy subjects. In the case of "It's All Gravy," the pull is between the personal/private/particular very real gravy and a universal and cosmic gravy.

DL: Certainly one of the characteristics of your poetry is the obvious joy you take in language. In this poem, you mix elevated diction with humble diction. Words like *cycads, luminiferous,* and *doulas* play up against words like *little brown specks, dumped in the sink,* and *Uncle Benny's pork-pie hat.* Talk about this disparity and fusion.

MS: The poem presented itself to me as both a personal poem, bursting with my own family history (Uncle Benny and my little brother's baby-talk), and a poem embracing the history of how humans have viewed the heavens. Aristotle, Newton, and Einstein on one side of the scale, and regular folks—a middle-class, suburban family, sitting down to dinner, to *a gravy with little brown specks.* I wanted the reader to experience both— *my gravy, your gravy, our gravy*—to know the gravy wasn't perfect, that it was made from scratch—and also to view it as something universal and cosmic. I realize now that these specks could be the planets sprayed across our solar system, or millions of stars spread across the Milky Way, but that double meaning was not my intention. That was a gift.

DL: I also admire your use of strategic repetition. The word *gravy*, for example, is used multiple times. Then you also use anaphora as in *splashes of milk of water of wine / let it cook let it thicken let it be spooned or poured // over bird over bovine over swine*. To my mind, such devices make the parts cohere and add music and momentum. Was that your intention or just a lucky outcome? Tell us how you went about working with repetition in this poem.

MS: There was quite a bit of luck in terms of how quickly this poem moved through the drafting process to completion, but the music and momentum were anything but luck, unless you count the luck of having an undergraduate instructor tell us to go home to our dorm rooms and recite all fifty-two sections of "Song of Myself." I was hoarse by section fifty-two, but I never again doubted the power of anaphora! Or the luck of hearing Allen Ginsberg read at Rutgers University in 1979 (my first poetry reading). If I had not adored Ginsberg's poem "America" these last thirty years, I do not think I would have had the nerve to use the word *gravy* fourteen times. Repetition comes naturally to me because I have had Whitman and Ginsberg singing in my brain since I was in my teens.

Bonus Prompt: The Word Chain Poem

Choose one word that you like the sound of. Be sure it has at least two syllables. Suggestions: purple, silver, yellow. I like colors because they immediately bring in the visual. But don't feel limited to colors.

Now put your word on the top line of your paper, all the way to the right.

Jumping off that lead word, quickly brainstorm a list of words with similar sounds. Avoid exact rhymes. One word per line. Each single word should lead to the next. Do not go back to the original word. If you include only words with the same initial sound, this will result in nice alliteration in the poem you write. But this is an option, not a requirement.

Example:

Purple
plump
plum
palm
plummet
pudding

Try to get at least ten words.

Now write a poem consisting of as many lines as you have words. Your first line will end with the first word in your list, the second line will end with the second word, and so on. Using the above example, line 1 will end with *purple*, line 2 will end with *plump*, and so on.

You should end up with a first draft that has some promising sounds, not exact rhymes but near rhymes.

III. Sound

*Painting is silent poetry, and
poetry is painting that speaks.*

—Plutarch

Craft Tip #7: Rhyme Your Way

—Kelly Cherry

My technical tip would once have been a simple assumption: Use rhyme. But these days, poets sometimes think it is stupid or sentimental to rhyme. It's not. When we think about rhyme, we often think about closure, but rhyme accomplishes many other things. It pulls the poem together. At the very least, a poem with echoes resonates longer than one without.

You can lighten your rhymes by varying line length or meter or by using partial rhymes, or slant rhymes, or sight rhymes. Or place your rhymes farther apart. Rhyme is malleable and musical and mnemonic. If you read carefully, you'll see that rhyme is used by quite a few contemporary poets. Robert Watson, Henry Taylor, and Michael Palma are a few who come quickly to mind. Anyone who reads the work of Annie Dillard will discover that she uses rhyme liberally and subtly to heighten emotion and drive home her points—even in nonfiction prose.

A poem is, among other things, the closest you can get in literature to music; rhyme can be as anxious and obsessive and possibly suffocating as a Shostakovich symphony or as transcendent as Bach and Beethoven. Who can afford to abandon such an extraordinary instrument?

Here's a rhyming trick that will add good sounds to your poem: From the first third of your poem, select one word. This can be an important word or an unimportant one. Then brainstorm a list of rhymes and near rhymes. Do that again in the middle third of your poem. And then in the final third. Now go back into the poem and see if you can plug in some of those words.

Here's another trick: Pull out that poem that has perfect end rhymes but falls short of pleasing you. Too sing-songy. Too predictable. For each second (or third or fourth) rhyme, find a word that's similar in sound and see if you can make some substitutions. For example, *handle* and *candle* might result in *handle* and *rekindle*. *Love* and *above* might result in *love* and *over*. You may need to make other changes in order to maintain sense, but the likelihood is that some of those changes will also improve your poem. Better sound. Better sense.

Poem and Prompt

Sonnenizio on a Line from Drayton

Since there's no help, come let us kiss and part; or kiss
anyway, let's start with that, with the kissing part,
because it's better than the parting part, isn't it—
we're good at kissing, we like how that part goes:
we part our lips, our mouths get near and nearer,
then we're close, my breasts, your chest, our bodies partway
to making love, so we might as well, part of me thinks—
the wrong part, I know, the bad part, but still
let's pretend we're at that party where we met
and scandalized everyone, remember that part? Hold me
like that again, unbutton my shirt, part of you
wants to I can tell, I'm touching that part and it says
yes, the ardent partisan, let it win you over,
it's hopeless, come, we'll kiss and part forever.

—Kim Addonizio

The *sonnenizio* is a form invented by Kim Addonizio. As its name suggests, the form is a spin-off of the sonnet.

Now for the rules:

1. Begin with a line borrowed from someone else's sonnet.

2. Select a single word from that line and repeat it in each subsequent line. Consider part of speech and different forms of the word, e.g., Addonizio's repeating word is *part,* but she

also uses *partway, party,* and *partisan.* She uses her word as noun, verb, and participle.

3. Have a total of 14 lines.

4. Make the last two lines rhyme.

Sample Poems

Sonnenizio on a Line from Yeats

You'd know the folly of being comforted
if you tried to comfort me with tired words
like *time* and *wounds* and *heal*: small comfort
when he's so comfortable jilting me
for the comforting embrace of his true love,
his joy, making the comforts of my bed
seem as soothing as Southern Comfort
on my birthday, drunk alone: sullen discomfort.
Still your attempts at comfort serve
as minor distraction, my tears no comfort,
my rage, my disbelief, my hurt comforting
no one. Revenge, though, would comfort me.
The revenge of living longer, the comfort
of love returned: comfort of the best sort.

—Claire Keyes
published in *Adanna Literary Journal*

Sonnenizio on a Willis Barnstone Line

The night is beautiful. I live alone
and listen to a lonesome howl beneath
a million lights. How could I be alone
when I'm alive, tuned to a Lone Star state
of mind? Some feel a loneliness out here,
my distant neighbor Malone, for instance,
who sits out front, a Lone Star in hand,
always alone, his fragile wife inside.
So he can leave his wife alone, nearby
a standalone refrigerator sits,
an exile on the porch, which I alone
witness. Malone does not appreciate
the night. A lone figure across the way—
is that how he sees me, alone and gray?

—Scott Wiggerman

Craft Tip #8: Sonic Imagination

—Baron Wormser

One of the questions that faces any poet is *Where do I find fresh words?* Shaping the language to one's own concerns always has been a hallmark of poetry, what a friend of mine calls *owning the dictionary*. Nonetheless, there are moments for any poet when the dull word stares back at the poet and mocks her or him. What to do?

For decades I have practiced what I call *sonic imagination*, which is to say I let sound lead me into word choices. I write, for instance, *Snow falls*. It's serviceable but to say that I have seen it before would be an understatement. What I do is take the letter that the dull verb begins with—*f*—and start writing down verbs that begin with that same letter. I don't make any judgment as I make my list. The whole point of inviting random words into one's poem is to allow the unconscious to go wherever it goes. Hence, *float, flutter, flit, flap, flicker, feint, fly, fumble, fake, flounce*, and *fail* present themselves. I can write ten words, twenty words, thirty words, forty words. Almost inevitably some word appears that I never would have reached otherwise, some word that both scintillates and fits in the poem.

Since the whole endeavor is based on trusting the unconscious, there is nothing suspect about doing this sort of mining. It's not so much brainstorming as imagination storming. There are a lot of verbs, adjectives, and nouns out there, to cite the three main parts of speech. I might as well access them.

One of the difficulties in writing free verse is that the rhythmic and sonic demands on the poet are less than in formal verse. One needs spurs to take poems to the places where they might go. Simple self-expression is not going to do that. Pushing sound is one way to get to those places. The soil of poetry is sound and rhythm. That applies mystically—the aural spell that poetry can weave—and practically—finding a better word than *falls*.

Poem and Prompt

American Supermarket Idyll

To go to America, to cruise the aisle of cereal choices forever,
that enormous aisle, long as a river.

To visit the produce department when the thunder
crashes and the rain mists down.

To discover unreal cheese, individually wrapped,
to peruse the lunch packs, meals already assembled.

To have to decide nothing, to have to decide
everything. To be handed plastic cups

of Spanish-style salmon from the woman
who cooks there, who gives you sponge cake too.

To take a cart for free and push it all day
if you want. To have to buy nothing. To have

to buy everything, to cruise three aisles
of frozen foods, never growing cold.

To roll broadly up to the checkout where cashiers are
always standing, where you never pack your own stuff.

To be asked Plastic or paper? Debit or credit?
Cash back? To go to the grocery store and come out

with more money in your pocket than when you went in.
To cruise the cereal choices forever.

—Suzanne Zweizig

Most likely the first thing you notice in this poem is the pattern of lines and sentences beginning with an infinitive, *To* followed by a verb. In the first stanza the speaker goes to a certain locale, here an American supermarket. She then proceeds to praise the virtues of the supermarket, its myriad challenges and wonders.

Notice that all stanzas are just two lines, so the pattern of repetition makes a drumbeat. But notice, too, that the poet varies the pattern in stanzas 5, 7, and 10. That's a smart move. Too much pattern leads to predictability and boredom.

To get started, pick a place to go to. You might begin with a country or a state or a city and then narrow down to a specific type of place. Include the location in your title, so you don't have to say it in the poem.

Begin with *To go to*—and keep on going. Worry about stanza breaks later

When the first infinitive seems to be tiring, bring in a new one, along with a new aspect of your location. Strive to capture the distinctive charactcristics and virtues of your place.

Fill up a full page.

Go over your draft, adding more material and crossing out the debris.

Now begin to work the material into two-line stanzas—or three, if you prefer.

Work with the infinitive pattern.

Several drafts in, be sure you've got some variety in your pattern.

Sample Poems

The Heart of Texas

To go to Texas, to wear Stetsons and cowboy boots
in the high state of fashion unlike Paris, on runways of dirt.

To ride white horses down the sandy beaches with Fabio,
or on dude ranches like *City Slickers* on a vacation from hell.

To hit the Houston Livestock Rodeo for the best rock concert,
peruse aisles of John Deere tractors. To shop the upscale area

one might compare to a Junior League Main Street Market,
minus the manure and hay you hope someone else steps on.

To get to the frothy beer and elephant ears, all you have to do
is take a deep breath; your salivary glands turn on, gushing

like the Guadalupe River, your mouth watering as you dream
of Galveston, oh Galveston. To Schlitterbahn or Moody
Gardens.

To sun on the beach as Fabio rides by on his horse; before
Matthew McConaughey rescues you just before the hurricane,

to ride off with a cowboy who touches you under the stars,
big and bright in the heart of Texas. To wear his Stetson hat.

—Laurie Kolp

Doctor Poets

To go to your desk, to write the poem
      that will cure cancer.

To open the drawer and pull out
      the stamps with American poets,

To remember Auden writing
      "poetry makes nothing happen,"

From years of chain smoking, his face lined
      with more craggy ridges than the Alps.

To stick the Wallace Stevens stamp
      on a self-sealing number ten envelope.

To grab the fresh legal pad marked "Evidence,"
      blue lines, white paper, three red lines

Making left margin markers, to think of *The Man*
      with the Blue Guitar, The Snow Man,

The Emperor of Ice Cream, The Idea of Order
      at Key West, Loneliness in Jersey City,

To gather up the words that will
      cure cancer as the letter C

By reciting from memory *The Comedian*
      as the Letter C, "Crispin at sea"?

To live longingly and outlandishly like Linus
      Pauling and his love affair with Vitamin C.

To offer the poem for free to all who need
      both a poem and a cure.

To survey the clutter and praise

the mess of your desk as your poem

Gets folded in three and tucked into its envelope
     with the Wallace Stevens stamp.

To address the envelope to the most likely editor
     who waits for it eagerly, SASE,

To accept it or reject it as the *Final Soliloquy*
     of the Interior Paramour

(Depending on whether or not she or he is cheery
     after a three martini lunch at 21)

And decides finally your poem not only cures cancer
     Thirteen ways but also the desperate needs

Of Mere Being and of pure being with the poem
     at the end of your mind.

—Sander Zulauf

Craft Tip #9: The Devotions of the Ear

—Jeffrey Levine

Long before I started writing, I was—and still am—a classical musician, having played the clarinet nearly all my life. Probably that's the source of my fascination with the connection between poetry and sound. After all, only half the job of being a musician is to turn sound into music. The other half of the work (the larger half, really) is to listen, whether while sitting (as the clarinets do) in the middle of the orchestra, surrounded by violins and cellos, violas, brass and percussion, or in the far more intimate setting of the chamber group, nearly alone on stage but for a small handful of other musicians, usually within arms' reach.

Making music is so much about connecting with other musicians; it's about listening intently to others as they, in turn, listen just as closely to you. The work is wordless, the gestures composed of sound and shaped by sound, by wind and the movement of fingers and bows. One communicates by example and reaction and with a certain extra-sensory *feel* for how sounds and silences fit together, climb, diminish, expand, express, pause, breathe.

Here's what I know. Fully realized poems come from the body and appeal to the body. Words talk to each other with the full range of sounds and silences that life's music contains and fails to contain, embraced at either end by the line (that grid that gives the sentence its shape, that puts sufficient pressure on the words within to come alive). There, in those lines, guided by the gods of specificity and the muses of sensory details (those nine still hard-at-it daughters of Zeus), it is sound that gives life to a poem, gives space to its contents, gives shape to its denizens, and animates time itself, the push and pull of it, the pell-mell of it, the marking time of it, the very feel of movement is conveyed though the device of sound. Artfully done, the sounds of the

71

line become the music of the line, and the music of the next line. They sing.

Here are a few lines from Charles Wright, found about midway through his poem, "A Journal of the Year of the Ox":

> Outside my door, a cicada turns its engine on.
> Above me the radar tower
> Tunes its invisible music in:
> > other urgencies tell their stories
>
> Constantly in their sleep,
> Other messages plague our ears
> > under Madonna's tongue:
> The twilight twists like a screw deeper into the west.

Spiritual, mystical, available, Wright's legacy as one of our most effective poets is earned in important part by his ear, which hears music and makes that music evident on the page. His ear pays close attention to the sounds and silences that are themselves the twin gods of music. Note how the sounds form the images, intensify them, and how the images make sound, intensify them. Note how sound, so closely heard, opens each image into surprise.

To hear deeply, we need to forget daily what we know of sound. Efface all expectation, every memory of what sounds sound like from our personal history. Think, for example, of the sound of a flute. Sweet. Metallic. Fluid. And then, hear the sound of Matt Malloy's flute, how it works against our expectations, how the sound is air and wood, becomes air, becomes wood itself.

As a clarinetist, I work day after day to perfect smooth ("legato") connections between one note and another. Finger control. Hand control. Breath control. One note should blend seamlessly into another, so that nobody hears the fingers or the in-between microtones as I move from one note to the next. This is hard enough to do when playing a "close interval"—two nearby notes. But it's devilishly difficult when there's a wider interval to bridge, and nearly impossible to perfect when the interval spans two or three of the clarinet's principal "registers."

Now to the flute playing of jazz musician Erik Lawrence. Sometimes he stops blowing altogether and instead uses his fingers, or rather, the pads of his fingers, slapping them down willfully upon the flute's keys and open holes in order to produce all of the sounds of the flute's scales and arpeggios. He even holds the flute up to the microphone so everything can be heard: not just the notes and the wind in them, but also the sound the fingers make, the sounds the pads make, and the mechanics of the flute's hardware (silverware). Lawrence knows that we'll hear completely fresh the tune and his improvisations on it, and the percussion and even the spaces between all of these sounds—the silences.

For every sound contains silence, every silence the intimation of sound. Writing is not, after all, about speaking. It's about listening. Write with the eyes closed, hear the sounds and silences with your outer ears and your inner ear, hear them as if for the first time, and be satisfied with no word and no line until you hear it sing.

Poem and Prompt

The Woodpecker Keeps Returning

The woodpecker keeps returning
to drill the house wall.
Put a pie plate over one place, he chooses another.

There is nothing good to eat there:
he has found in the house
a resonant billboard to post his intentions,
his voluble strength as provider.

But where is the female he drums for? Where?

I ask this, who am myself the ruined siding,
the handsome red-capped bird, the missing mate.

—Jane Hirshfield

This poem is initially deceptively simple, then takes on increasing complexity. The question and its one-word reiteration mark a kind of turn in the poem. Suddenly, the poem is no longer about the bird but is about the speaker who identifies with the bird as well as with the house he pecks. The poem transcends literal description and moves to metaphor.

Choose one of Nature's creatures. Perhaps another kind of bird or a worm, a groundhog, a mouse. Then begin with simple description of what your creature is doing. Keep the action simple as it is in Hirshfield's poem.

Let a question come in. See what that leads to. Perhaps to a metaphor?

Sample Poems

Moose Sighting at Sunrise

The juvenile moose ambles across
Rte. 8 to catch up with its mother
patient among thick pines
on Searsburg Mountain's west slope.
They ascend with ease, stopping
when a lesson is needed
that life is but one long trail of obstacles
to overcome, and which to walk away from.
Mother and calf navigate upstream through
falling water and glint of the rising sun
to a meal of new-growth
saplings at the base of the windmills
which churn atop the ridgeline
and accompany the cascading
water and low hum of turbine.
We used to hike here
where you always hoped to see moose.
Why aren't you here?
If you hadn't given up
on us, you'd have seen it too.

—Bill Wunder

The Cerberus Puppy School Trainer Takes Us on a Tour

Look at this one, a palisade of thorny baby
teeth protruding from his gums,

or that one, mouth gaping, hackles of coarsened
hair riding the bony ridges of his back.

But of course, that's all prop, like our motto:
Three heads are better than one.

It's in home-training where they learn the real
stuff: the meaning of the fence,

the sin inside a sleeve, the way to ravage hems
and rug-fringe,

the presumptuous fingers of those ever-present
fawning hands.

We drill into our dogs a sense that mastication
is an art,

a talent for the rending of false margins. We tell
them that *dismember*

means to forget, that flesh can be crossed like
the banks of a river.

—Jeanne Wagner
published in *Atlanta Review*

The Poet on the Poem: Edward Byrne

After the Miscarriage

Before breakfast, passing below the blank
      windows of lovers' hotel rooms, we walked

toward the harbor. At the end of a steep
      cobblestone street, we could see the water's

edge, its morning mist still lifting
      like a vague gray veil and dissipating

as if in some deliberate act of abandonment,
      although the horizon line was yet nowhere

to be seen. A few boys in black coats
      huddled together against the still chilly

spring weather. Beside the low wall
      along the wharf that now seemed bleached

white by an early light, hands cupped
      for shelter from the wind, they smoked

cigarettes and spoke of last evening's
      adventures—once more told those lies

they'd told before. Alone among rows
      of umbrellaless cafe tables, you wrote

notes home on a picture postcard
      addressed to your sister, while I bought

fresh fruit and flowers at the market,
      even though I could not find the yellow

roses you'd hoped would brighten
       our rented brownstone apartment.

Returning, we moved through the public
       park, its thin trees and clusters of lilac

shrubs just beginning to bud, its large
       garden plots already filling with color.

As we followed the red brick path
       all around a reflecting pool, we listened

to the shrill whistle of an overnight
       train finally arriving at the railway

terminal, and we heard the slow toll
       of cathedral bells calling parishioners

for morning Mass, both of us believing
       each sound offered its own form of warning.

DL: The title of this poem is a good example of the power a title can have. Yours colors the reader's understanding of, and emotional response to, the poem. Did it come before or after you wrote the poem? Did you set out to write a poem about a miscarriage?

EB: I never decide upon a title for a poem before the end of writing a first draft, especially because my method of writing does not allow for me to know what the poem will concern until I am somewhat into the process of composition. I almost always begin with only an image or phrase that I regard as interesting, which initiates a discovery of other lines describing scenes and actions, one leading to another. I remember that this poem began with the following simple thought and straightforward opening statement: *Below windows of hotel rooms, we walked toward the harbor.*

My poems often begin with an image or incident, seek out a conflict, and arrive at a resolution, whether stated or suggested by the close of the poem. When I wrote this poem, I didn't know what the topic would be until I was two-thirds of the way through the original draft. At that point I realized I was wondering about the emotional state of a couple that has felt a sense of loss.

The poem is not autobiographical or documentary. After it was published, my wife had to assure friends and relatives that she'd not kept from them the secret of a miscarriage. Instead, I drew inspiration from those I have known who have been through such a situation. I also considered how my parents might have felt after a sister of mine died in her infancy when I was young. In addition, I might have been reflecting an emotion felt when my own son was diagnosed with autism— representing an initial awareness parents of autistic children often experience, that the individual they had envisioned growing up and inhabiting a certain kind of imagined future had somehow been taken away from them.

DL: In addition to the work done by the title, your details provide an understory, a sub-text. For example, *boys in black coats, Shrill whistle, slow toll / of cathedral bells, morning Mass,* and *its own form of warning* convey an untold story and heighten the emotional intensity. How do you manage to balance the lyric and narrative impulses?

EB: My style of writing seems to naturally combine lyric language and ingredients of narrative or implied narrative subtexts. I feel comfortable with this mixture. I intend that the two parts complement one another. Most of the details you mention were added in revisions after I had established the context of the poem, and each was inserted in order to create an ambiance supporting the subject matter or as a contrast to the position in which the couple find themselves.

My personal history includes an interest in film studies. When watching films, I'm always conscious of the many minor components within the frame of the screen. Directors making movies are aware of the contribution subtle background atmosphere (natural scenery, weather, sounds, actions, set decorations, and extra actors populating the area) can add to a film moment's dramatic tension and emotional tone, even offering possible undercurrents or sub-plots. In my poetry I try to think cinematically and inject images or elements evoking various senses, as well as objects that mirror the kind of attention to detail I observe in effective movie scenes.

DL: What attracts you to the two-line stanza?

EB: I have always believed the opening and closing lines of stanzas receive added attention from readers, and perhaps this form similarly forces such a concentrated focus on each line in the poem. Also, since my lines tend to be longer, the added white space between the many couplets serves to lessen the weight the poem might appear to have if the stanzas were shaped into large black blocks of print. I like to think of the stanza breaks as the leaven, substances that lift or transform what otherwise could be a heavy and doughy passage burdening the poetry.

I like the way the two-step form gives an illusion of order and a feeling of regular pacing throughout the poem, while the language remains a more relaxed and familiar free verse, presenting a tension between an apparently arranged stanza pattern and the casual flexibility within the lines. I am a big fan of jazz musicians, particularly those figures from the bebop era who used riffs from a standard song as a starting point around which they improvised and wound inventive solos. I like to think that in a small way the free verse two-step stanza imitates that method.

DL: Tell us about your use of syllabics.

EB: In the past I would write first drafts of poems in syllabic form: for instance, counting 8 or 9 or 10 syllables per line, sometimes simply for fun as an exercise. Then in the revisions I would add or subtract syllables as I sought more exact words or inserted more lyrical choices. Therefore, the final draft would contain only a rough resemblance to the strict syllabics in the original version. Still, the ghostly sense of syllabic form would somehow remain when readers encountered the poem.

In fact, even though I didn't attempt to preserve the syllabics, and I thought the lines in final drafts always varied from the initial composition, occasionally the syllabic pattern would withstand the revisions. When one of my colleagues once asked me about a poem in one of my books that he taught to his class as an example of syllabic form, I had to confide to him that I was surprised because I thought I'd lost the true syllabic form when I had made many emendations in revision. In fact, I'd never counted the syllables after the first draft and didn't realize the syllabic count had survived my revisions.

DL: You have a wonderful ear for the music in language. I find internal rhyme, near rhyme, assonance, consonance, and alliteration. To what extent do you labor to make use of such sonic devices? At what stage in your drafting do they enter in?

EB: If there were an aspect of my poetry that I find myself enjoying the most, the musicality of the work would be a primary candidate. As you indicate, I like to employ various devices that more subtly assimilate sound as a central element. I enjoy adding onomatopoeic words as well.

I'm also aware of purposely trying to have the speaker's voice group together similar sounding words or phrases and use vowels or consonants that imitate the tone of the content in the poem, perhaps contemplative or combative—whether with soothing softer sounds or the introduction of harder and harsher notes. Again thinking cinematically, I compare such an aural motif to soundtrack music that echoes the mood in a movie.

I regularly remind my students that writers must love words for their denotative meanings and connotative suggestions, as well as for their historic or cultural associations. I know I do. Moreover, they should be prepared to exploit the musicality of the language, appealing to the ear as well as the eye. If our selections are accurate and effective, each facet of the perfect word in any line of a poem could contribute to the overall goal of evoking emotional and intellectual responses from readers.

Bonus Prompt: The Well-Dressed Poem

Make a list of articles of clothing that hold some significance for you. Make them very specific, e.g., your first prom dress, your wedding dress, your father's red plaid flannel shirt, the nightgown you wore on your honeymoon, your football jersey.

Choose one and freewrite about it. Give yourself 5-10 minutes. No pausing to think. Don't bother to be fancy or poetic.

Now rewrite the piece from the point of view of the article. Let the article of clothing be the first person speaker. What does the dress remember? How'd that shirt feel going off to the Salvation Army?

In subsequent drafts, turn your piece into a poem.

IV. Voice

If you want to move your reader, write more coldly.

—Anton Chekov

Craft Tip #10: Voice Lessons

—Kathryn Stripling Byer

I grew up wanting to be a singer. I sang solos in church. I sang to the cows in the pastures. I sang quietly into the window of the bus as it made its long journey home from school every afternoon. Neither the window nor the cows gave me stage fright. Singing solo in church did. Would my voice be there? What would I hear? Anything at all? Remembering my anxiety as I opened my mouth to begin "In the Garden," I recall Fred Chappell's comment that the blank, mute page makes every honest writer feel a surge of doubt. Even opera singers confess to an occasional loss of voice that renders them unable to sing what was once their signature arias.

Like most young poets I worried about *finding my voice*. Now in middle age, after serving for five years as North Carolina's Poet Laureate, concentrating more on a public voice than my inner one, I worry about finding it again.

Reading soprano Renée Fleming's memoir, *The Inner Voice: The Making of a Singer*, set me wondering about what advice she might give. Maybe she would tell me I ought to take this mystery of voice literally. Maybe I should try to think of voice as a real singer might. *Stop worrying about having lost your voice and start singing,* she might suggest. *Try singing your own lines from earlier poems when you were in voice, even if only as recitative and not aria. Really hear those lines, bodily, in every part of you.*

She might then add, *Oh, and by the way, sing along with the CD player while driving. If you keep punching back to a song numerous times because you love the way it feels in your ear and in your mouth, you are onto something important. Take the song that makes your hair stand on end and write from it, generating words that rise out of the song's lyrics.*

I took Fleming's imagined advice. On walks, I'd sing, quietly, lines from my poems, when I was sure nobody else was around. In the car I sang along with Etta James, Nina Simone, and even Renée herself in her *Dark Hope* album. Driving back over the Blue Ridge mountains, I listened to Dolly Parton's version of "Silver Dagger" from her bluegrass collection. I listened to it over and over again, goose bumps rising on my arms every time, and when I got home, I began singing it onto the page, letting the first word of the song become the title.

Don't

sing love songs to me
lest you waken the blade

that seeks marrow, my heart's
muscle, bone-chain

that carries me deep
into shady groves where

I hear naught but my own
blood dissembling.

I hadn't a clue where this poem was going, where this woman's voice was leading my own, but lead me it did.

The impetus of language approximating the original lyrics worked poetic magic: I suddenly heard wildflower names bursting through, along with words like *reft* and *dissembling* that I'd never used in a poem before. I heard—no, I *felt* my *voice* cracking the whip, a live wire again. Living as I do in the Blue Ridge mountains, I find that old ballads and folk songs wield special power for me, but jazz and blues do, too. I'm sure that Nina Simone's "Lilac Wine" is waiting for a poem.

Wait a minute, though. If I'm going to continue to work on voice like a real singer, I have to practice, don't I? I can see

86

Madame Fleming nodding her head, like my piano teacher, who once told me I didn't practice hard enough. One of the best ideas I've heard lately came from a renowned pianist who described his daily practice as playing the same Mozart sonata, finding something to learn from it each day.

Why not come back every day to a poem that has stirred us, reading it aloud, learning it by heart, listening to its inner voice over and over again? Our own voices will respond to that voice, taking shape on the page, in our mouths, in our ears. After all, voices long to sing back to other voices. My Inner Diva's advice? Let them.

Poem and Prompt

After

All long labors, whether for hunger, for duty, for
Pleasure, or none of the above, one day wrap up.
Put down the itinerant's beaten pouch, pluck no fruit further;
Linger over the melancholy taste of last on the tongue.
Even a switchblade wit can't sever another stem.

Plenty is a relative measure—if less than paradise,
It's more than enough. The prolific orchard will of course
Continue, other soles trod ladders into the heady
Kingdom of weighted boughs. Insatiable, you might even say
Incorrigible (as though mumbling in winter sleep), the way they can't
Not keep coming back, grasping, tugging, lifting down those
Globes that swell and blush to be handled so.

—Jeanne Marie Beaumont

Read the poem and see if you can identify its form.

If you said *acrostic*, you've got it. Most of the acrostic poems we find are done in elementary school classrooms. Beaumont demonstrates that it's possible to do an acrostic poem that has substance. Notice that she's chosen as her guide words the title of Robert Frost's poem, "After Apple-Picking." This immediately gives the poem some texture as it now carries the ghost of Frost's poem. In her poem Beaumont revisits Frost's subject matter and makes subtle allusions to his poem.

For your own guide words, use the title of a published poem. Choose a poem that calls for some kind of response. Maybe there's another side of the story that needs to be told. Maybe the original poem needs to be updated. Maybe there's a different gender perspective. Go back and carefully reread the poem. You want it to influence your own new poem.

Beaumont has used one of her words as the title of her poem. You might choose to do the same or not. Now put your words down the left margin, one letter per line.

Begin your first line, letting the letter guide you. Move to the next line and so on. The pitfall here is lapsing into triviality in order to get a line. Let that happen for the time being. Or feel free to leave a line empty.

Once you have a draft, go back and fill in the empty spaces. Don't allow any weak lines to linger. Keep working to make each line as strong as your best line. Work hard on the diction. Don't settle for the first words that came to you. Notice Beaumont's use of strong words: *itinerant, melancholy, switchblade, insatiable, incorrigible, globes.*

Pay attention to the music in Beaumont's poem. Read the poem aloud. Notice the alliteration of *long labors, pouch* and *pluck, fruit further.* Notice the assonance of *hunger, duty, none of the above, one, up.* Now go through your poem and replace flat words with ones that offer music as well as meaning.

Sample Poems

In a Station

One NY subway stop looks like another looks like another.
F train, E train, D train, C train—grab a seat, stand clear of

The closing doors—"We're being held in the station"—
Ha! No kidding!—"We should be moving shortly"—*Should*
Expresses what's expected. *Shortly* is subway-speak,

Meaning anything—five seconds—five minutes.
Everybody waits like moss on a log. You know the movie
The Taking of Pelham One Two Three, the original, not the
Remake with Denzel Washington and John Travolta?
Outstanding MTA! The pride of the city! I love fiction.

—Joel Allegretti

Rosebuds Ungathered

Though Herrick advised that marriage and its pleasures be goals
Of youthful females, untouched and barren while bereft of men,

The rosebud, then and still, reflects chances missed, treasures lost:
Hearty kisses, sunflowers, a walk along a foaming beach—
Examples less poignant than the maternity nurse, no Herrick

Virgin but a wife who'd borne three or four, all still at home.
In winter she'd brought the newborn to his mother who'd been
Regaled with gifts—blue sweater, cap, and booties crafted by
Great Aunt Lily. And a Whitman's Sampler, nougats, cherries
In labeled pockets. *Take one,* said the nursing mother. The plump
Nurse, tempted, said, *I'm on a diet*, denied herself one small treat,
Started home, thinking of sweets as her car slid off the icy road.

—Gail Fishman Gerwin

Craft Tip #11: How Do You Know This Voice Is Your Own?

—Lola Haskins

I'll start with a caveat. Consciously imitating the style of people you admire makes a lot of sense and almost all of us who are serious about poetry have written lots of imitations because we know that's how you learn. Besides, copying the masters is a time-honored tradition in not just painting but any art form. Django, my thirty-eight-year-old singer-songwriter son, for instance, consciously copied the styles of groups he admired for maybe ten years before he thought he was ready to strike out on his own. During that time, when I'd say, *X is a really great song*, he'd come back with, *It's not really mine; I'm just figuring out how it was done.*"

If you're going to claim a poem that started with someone else's, you have to purge it of its original impulse. If imitation inspired your piece, start by pruning it of imitative material and keep at it until every leaf is yours. After that, check your line lengths and structure to be sure what you're using reflects the pace *you* intend for this poem, as opposed to the pace the poem you started out with was keeping. This step sometimes slips by and it's important.

Once that's done, make the poem even more yours by cutting any words you wouldn't use yourself and also by seeing if you can substitute interesting/personal words for any generic/lazy verbs that happen to be lying around not doing much. Your substitutions need to be carefully chosen, though. If you're naturally plain-spoken, for example, you want those words to be plain, too. You definitely in any case need to be careful you're not using words to show off unless you actually want your voice to sound pretentious.

If your poem started on its own rather than from bouncing off someone else's, a lot of what I've just said still applies. Often drafts of poems aren't full-voiced but more like templates for what you may originally have had in mind (bear in mind that that may have changed), so to make sure they're in your own personal voice and style, you'll need—at a minimum—to go through the pruning and enhancing steps. And before you decide the poem is finished, go back and make sure it doesn't leave anything out that you know but the reader wouldn't.

Here's the bottom line, as I see it. You're entitled to call a poem your own, meaning it's officially in your voice, when:

1. you've deleted all trace of your original inspiration (if the poem began imitatively)
2. there are no editorial or format changes left to make
3. it sings the way *you* sing
4. no one but you could have written it

Poem and Prompt

Post Hoc

It happened because he looked a gift horse in the mouth.
It happened because he couldn't get that monkey off his back.
It happened because she didn't chew 22 times before swallowing.
What was she thinking, letting him walk home alone from the bus stop?
What was he thinking, standing up in the boat like that?
Once she signed those papers the die was cast.
She should have waited an hour before going in; everyone knows
salami and seawater don't mix.
He should have checked his parachute a seventh time;
you can never be too careful.
Why didn't she declare her true feelings?
Why didn't she play hard to get? She could be out at some
nice restaurant right now instead of in church, praying
for the strength to let him go.
It all started with that tattoo.
It all started with her decision to order the chicken salad.
Why was he so picky?
Why wasn't she more discriminating?
He should have read the writing on the wall; listened
to the still small voice, had a lick of sense. But how could he when he
was blinded by passion? Deaf to warnings? Really dumb?
Why, why, in God's name, did he run with scissors?
If only they'd asked Jesus for help.
If only they'd asked their friends for help.
If only they'd ignored the advice of others and held fast
to their own convictions, they might all be here, now,
with us, instead of six feet under; instead of trying to adopt
that foreign baby, instead of warming that barstool
at the Road Not Taken Eatery and Lounge, wondering how it might all
have been different, if only they had done
the right thing.

—Jennifer Maier

You should have a good time with this one. Notice, first, the use of clichés. Aren't we supposed to avoid them? Yes, but if we can refurbish them as Maier has, then they work. Notice also some pieces of advice scattered throughout the poem. And the use of anaphora. And the alternation of questions with declarative sentences.

Now quickly brainstorm a list of clichés.

Next, quickly brainstorm a list of pieces of advice you've received or given.

Using the material from your two lists, begin to draft your poem. Use a third person speaker and have two people in the poem.

Use at least three different repeated sentence beginnings to give the poem lots of anaphora.

Use lots of questions and alternate them with declarative sentences.

Go over your draft and revise and revise until the poem is truly your own. You might use stanzas, add some rhyme, change the point of view.

The title, *Post Hoc*, means the fallacy of assuming that temporal succession is evidence of causal relation. You might use a different Latin phrase as your title.

Sample Poems

Carpe Diem

Try to seize a day.
As luck would have it, that is a row too long to hoe.
Why do people try, time after time?

Why does my doctor keep telling me
to lose weight, exercise more, avoid stress?
There's no time like the present, he says.
All in due time, I reply.

Why do my graduate students ask,
What do we need to do for an A?
Connection and reproduction.
Dissolution and destruction.
Do your homework.

One girl, the spitting image of my college girlfriend, asks,
Why is love blind?
Life is a bowl of cherries, my dear, fall
in love, have sex, die a little, love again.
It's give and take.

A boy who doesn't have both oars in the water, asks me,
How should we lead our lives?
Promote life figuratively and literally.
Follow the Silk Road. Lie down in the heather.

But you're as old as dirt, over the hill, long in the tooth,
says a hard-headed boy with a face only a mother could love.
He gets under my skin.

I have seen him outside class drunk as a skunk,
smoking cigarettes with Destrudo and Libido—
such cruel knowledge they possess.

Time heals no wounds.
But it's the eleventh hour and time is running out.
Each minute, a small death on the tip of my tongue.

—Kenneth Ronkowitz

Water Over the Dam

To be fair, he had it coming
To be fair, he hadn't a clue
To be fair, he never saw it coming

She was a knockout, a bombshell

To be fair, she thought he was her soul mate
To be fair, she could learn to forget and forgive
Truth be told, she didn't put her feet where her mouth was

Hers was the face that launched a thousand ships

All the tea in China couldn't bring him back
He wouldn't return if his life depended on it
He wouldn't stoop that low

She could eat her heart out and he'd be none the wiser

Before she was a gleam in her father's eye, she'd loved him
Before Adam made Eve, he'd loved her
Love means never having to say you're sorry

He could lie through his teeth and she'd be none the wiser

What was he thinking, living as though there were no tomorrow
How do you let someone just slip through your fingers like that
He wasn't worth it anyway, she wasn't worth it anyway

There are plenty more fish in the sea

—Ingrid Wendt

Craft Tip #12: Some Uses of Myth

—Linda Pastan

Penelope

The sun is scarcely
a shadow of itself,
it bled into the sea
all last week
and now, bandaged away,
waits out with me the long, long
month of rain.

Grey fades to grey.
The horizon is
the finest seam between
water and water, sky and sky.
Only the tide still moves,
leaving the print of its ribbed bones
on the abandoned sand
as you left yours on me
when you moved imperceptibly from my embrace.

I must wring out the towels,
wring out the swimsuits,
wring my eyes dry of tears,
watching at a window
on one leg, then the other,
like the almost extinct heron.

"Penelope" is a poem I started one summer, my husband away
for a week, as I stared out at the Atlantic and felt lonely and
sorry for myself. The result was not so much sentimental as
self-indulgent—two sides of the same coin. Then, during one of
those wonderful, if rare, moments of insight, it occurred to me

that Penelope herself must have stood in much the same way I was standing, her husband also gone, looking out at a very different body of water.

I decided I would call my poem "Penelope." While I kept it in the first person and didn't change anything but the title, a sudden distance was created between me, Linda Pastan, and the woman speaking the poem. A universal quality was added, as if by magic, to words that would otherwise have been simply personal.

Since that time, Penelope has become a sort of second self (I have written dozens of poems in her name) as have Eve, Daphne, Gretel, even Dido (though I never contemplated suicide myself). Using figures from story or myth can add depth to a poem and, like changing the voice from the first to the third person, the perception of objectivity.

And it can also help when one's own creative well is running dry. Think of a favorite fable or myth, use it as the basis for any kind of poem you want to write, and suddenly there will be a wealth of material for you to turn to.

Poem and Prompt

Curse: After Archilochus

With luck you'll get lost in some
tough neighborhood, caught
in a traffic of piranhas
and squeegee men with rags
full of acid. With luck gangbangers
will batter your fenders to tinfoil,
pull you through the window,
and teach you the fine arts
of suffering, then leave you,
a lump, in the gutter.
May you lie there, blood crusting
your lips, bruises decorating
your torso like tattoos.
May ice descend from the winter sky
making your teeth rattle to crumbs—
a dog whipped in the worst way.
With luck I'll be nearby to witness such glory
for all the evil you've done to me.

—Vern Rutsala

Rutsala writes in the ancient poetic tradition of the curse poem. Although he does not identify the recipient of the speaker's wrath, by using apostrophe, that is, direct address, he gives a personal feel to the poem and offers the reader of the poem the pleasure of eavesdropping.

The poetry here is subtle, but it's here. Notice the images, the circular structure (the repetition of *With luck*), metaphors, compression, and strong diction.

Make a quick list of people, creatures, or objects that have made you angry, really angry. The dog that terrified you or your child, the thief who stole your purse, the car that wouldn't start, the lover who betrayed you, the teacher who humiliated you.

From your list make one selection.

You may identify the recipient of your speaker's wrath and/or the nature of the grievance, or you may hold back that information. If you want to identify, the title might be a good place for that. Or you might plant clues throughout the poem. But keep the emphasis on the curse, and leave room for mystery.

Then freewrite, fast and furious, without a lot of thinking or worrying about whether or not you dare say this. Just say it. Make your first draft at least twice as long as the model poem.

In your revision, condense down to your best lines. Then go through the poem line by line and make the diction more forceful.

Notice the use of fairly short lines. That seems perfect for a poem that appears to be an outpouring of emotion. If your poem is longer and if you want breathing space, time to gather steam, consider using more than one stanza.

Sample Poems

Curse of the Three-Hour Ride

May you get lost on some back road
that leads into a swamp filled with
quicksand and I am there gloating
as you get sucked under, begging
for someone to toss you a rope.
May you sink slowly, muck clogging
your windpipe, legs useless, your chest
about to implode, remember
how you and your partner intent
on avoiding roads with stoplights
for hours trapped me in your Volvo,
my poor torqued back rigid with pain,
as you bounced along those rutted
farm lanes high-fiving each other.
May you die knowing your fate's not
by my hand, this final back road
all your own doing. I'll not shed a tear.

—Nancy Scott

103

Lucifer Is Your BFF

You will attain everything you ever desired,
and it will bring you emptiness.
You will watch your children choose
to grow away from you and your heart
will feel the strand of love sever
like a piano wire, and you will bleed, yes,
you will bleed with the tacit knowledge
that nothing you do will stop the flow.

Fresh wrongs will find you, point you out
in a crowd like a child fingering her abuser,
and you will be the wolverine
who does not remember its trail
of blood lust, and thus you will live
a long life in painful confusion.

You will age gracelessly, fold
rather than wrinkle, your bones will ache
and illness will burn in your lungs,
flamed by every waking breath
and each germ will become a disease
for which there is no name or cure.

And I will make it a point not to forgive you,
to remember every vile act, every mean
word, and when I think of you,
I will imagine a snow globe, you seated
on a bench in the center, and when I shake it,
I will watch razor-sharp flakes whittle you away.

—Donna Pflueger

The Poet on the Poem: Jan Beatty

Stray

a guy in a john deere hat tells the reporter: he was quiet,
a good neighbor. he took good care of his yard. then we see his body,
sunken in on itself. hair hanging down. feet lurching inches at a time

in shackles. sometimes I look at people and think: I can feel the blade
of your little machinery. turning inside you from some generator.
cutting you off from yourself. no trace of the older couple down the street,

their bodies he sliced to bits. up the cement ramp to the county jail,
he looks down. pieces of skin still under his fingernails but nothing
we can see. I think: look at his undiscovered cities. the buildings rising

in him and their fierce armies. you can't tell how he packaged them
in 6-inch squares, to be sent through the mail. christmas presents
to the family. now the woman next door: he made good potato salad.

brought it to church functions. standing in her yard, she looks down.
imagines his big hands in the dark blades of her grass/sees him cutting
the vegetables next to her daughter in the social hall. newly afraid,

she looks out into the camera: this is a good neighborhood. nothing
like this ever happens here. if someone strays from themselves,
does it turn the good in them to dust? here's what I know: we don't want

any trouble. what if he was split off from all kindness from the beginning?
I think: you are all little frankensteins: all little broken-down machines.
you put your head down. one foot in front of the other. lurching.

DL: There's a grisly story in this poem, a neighborhood shattered by an act of violence. There are also some odd moments of something like tenderness—*his undiscovered cities. the buildings rising / in him* and the *potato salad.* How much is fact? How much invention?

JB: That's a hard question to answer. The entire poem is sort of a composite of real things that happened over time, but not as one event. So the events did happen, in a sense, but not in any logical, grounded way. And yes, there is some invention in the making of the composite, and I have taken some liberties with some details. The reference to the *potato salad* was a sarcastic moment in the poem, referring to the moment on the news when the neighbor seems to be clueless, offering proof of goodness based on someone's cooking ability. The *undiscovered cities* is a moment of compassion and wondering in the poem.

DL: This poem reminds me of a braid. The way you weave together voices and perspectives both complicates and enriches the poem. The reader has to pay careful attention and do some work to keep track of who's speaking or whose thoughts we're hearing. How do you strike the balance between clarity and complication?

JB: I do intend for the reader to have to keep track of these voices and thoughts. I think that there are enough connections in the poem to do that, and in that connecting, I was hoping to spark moments of unexpected misunderstandings and wanderings of thought. It's not so essential to me that the reader *get* what I was intending, in terms of meaning, but that he/she is moved or affected by the poem. I do, though, want enough clarity to find a reading, to arrive at a kind of sense. I'm not interested in creating a poem that is intentionally opaque or misleading.

DL: The elegant form of the poem seems at odds with the chaos of the narrative. I love that irony and tension. Tell us how you arrived at the form. How many drafts until you arrived at the final form?

JB: This poem lived through many drafts—I don't remember how many, but more than ten. It initially was not in tercets, was not lower case, had a different title, was more traditionally narrative. The poets Judith Vollmer and Peter Oresick worked with me on an early draft of the poem. The poem needed to get tougher and less compassionate than it originally was—it needed more of an edge. I was formerly a social worker, and I worked and taught in prisons. Some of that experience goes into this poem as the poem straddles moments of toughness and tenderness.

DL: You use four stylistic devices that intrigue me. Could you comment on each of the following:

1. the absence of capital letters

JB: I think because of the stray voice speaking the poem, the stray voices that respond as neighbors, the stray voices inside all of us, I wanted to have the lower-case throughout the poem to support that feeling of a floating voice. Also, the lower case supports the movement of the poem through open stanzas and prevents any visual distractions during that movement.

2. the use of colons (I've counted eight of them.)

I used the colons to support the reporting voice in the poem, to move abruptly from voice to voice, as in, ... *now the woman next door:* ... The colon allows me to announce her appearance and to have her speak quickly in the poem. It is a bit rougher than a comma, which is want I wanted, to go along with the tone of the poem.

3. the use of italics

I used the italics to denote speech and internal thought. Usually, I would make a distinction in a poem between how those two are handled—for example, using quotes for speech, italics for unspoken thought. But in this poem, I wanted the unspoken and spoken to meet, to sort of speak to each other.

107

The poem is addressing what is said and isn't said, and for that reason, I wanted them to appear with the same notation.

4. the slash mark in stanza 5 (*grass/sees*), a device you use only once in this poem but more liberally in other poems

I used the slash at that place because it's a pivotal moment in the poem. Prior to that, we see a *blade* in stanza 2, a *sliced* in stanza 3, and by the time we get to that moment in stanza 5 when the woman envisions this man's hands in *blades of grass*, the emotional weight of those words has grown. It's at that moment that we as readers witness her uncomfortable realization that rushes on her: she knows this man, she starts to panic, to imagine his hands in the *blades*, and then she jumps quickly to *him cutting the vegetables next to her daughter*. It's at that moment when the terror sets in, when it gets personal, and she starts to question her position. So the slash between the *grass/sees* enables that jump, that shift, and vaults the reader and the language ahead to the moment of change.

DL: I'm also intrigued by the voice and tone of this poem. What is the speaker's relationship to the other characters? Is she one of them or separate from them? Why does she conclude, *you are all little frankensteins: all little broken-down machines*?

JB: She is one of them, and she is separate from them. She understands them, yet she reports on them. She witnesses the walk and the talk, and at the end, she is still all of them, raising questions and making statements. She is asking for compassion in *what if he was split off from all kindness from the beginning?* She is splitting off from *them* as she says, *you are all little frankensteins...* I guess that's the point of the poem—how and where do we locate ourselves in relation to the *other*? Don't we all stray? How does that process of locating shift? Then who are we, really? The questions are posed, not answered.

Bonus Prompt: The Negative Inversion Poem

Take a poem by someone else, place it on your writing surface, and add a blank piece of paper to the right or left of the poem.

Go to the first line. Then on your fresh piece of paper, write the opposite of that line. For example, next to *How do I love thee? Let me count the ways*, you might write: *You know how I detest you. I need not enumerate.*

Do this with each line. You may find a serious tug at some point. Feel free to go with it. After you've run out of steam, return to the host poem and pick up where you left off.

Revise as needed. Revise some more. Don't remove the sweet surprises. Trust them.

Comb the poem for weak diction. Make it better.

This prompt can be repeated endlessly. You should never again find yourself with a day when you have nothing to write about.

This activity can also be used with one of your own poems, perhaps one that never took on life.

V. Imagery / Figurative Language

Don't tell me the moon is shining;
show me the glint of light on broken glass.

- Anton Chekhov

Craft Tip #13: Petals on a Wet, Black Bough

—Adele Kenny

In a Station of the Metro

The apparition of these faces in the crowd;
Petals on a wet, black bough.

—Ezra Pound

What is it about Pound's poem that captures the imagination? It's a short poem, only two lines, and it *says* little. There are only two images in this poem—the apparition of the faces and the tree petals to which those faces are compared. However, Pound evokes thoughts about attraction, human beauty, and springtime; we feel his surprise and awe. He might have written, *I stepped into the metro and saw faces in the crowd that looked like tree blossoms.* The haunting quality and the heart of Pound's words are powered by a fundamental component of poetry—imagery.

Imagery is best explained as vivid description or figures of speech used to recreate things seen (or otherwise perceived) through written language. Imagery is often explained as the process of creating mind pictures with words, but, while image is synonymous with picture, effective imagery is not exclusively visual and may spark any of the senses. Imagery enhances meaning, develops tone, enriches context, creates tension, and establishes voice. It can also be a means through which a poet reveals a poem's emotional center.

In my work with poets in workshops and critiquing sessions, I offer the following suggestions for creating successful images:

1. Always be specific, avoid general terms, phrases, and statements. Images aren't about abstractions or philosophical

musings. Rather, they evoke the meaning and truth of human experiences in perceptible and actual terms.

2. Avoid lofty language and literary affectation. Neither big words nor literary pretensions lend themselves well to effective imagery. The imagery *wow factor* lies in language that is unexpected and deceptively simple.

3. Watch out for clichéd images. Examine your poems carefully and note any phrases or lines that seem familiar or general. Work to create images that are striking and fresh— distinctive and different. Think in terms of similes, metaphors, and other types of figurative language, and how you can use these to enhance your images. W. H. Auden said that a poem *must say something significant about a reality common to us all, but perceived from a unique perspective.* That unique perspective can be articulated through imagery.

4. Don't merely *ornament* your poems with images. Good imagery isn't a pair of Louboutin shoes or a Rolex watch. Imagery doesn't *dress up* a poem and should only be used to present your subject exactly as you perceive it. Imagery that's too deliberate or self-consciously *poetical* can ruin an otherwise good poem. Don't be clever or cutesy. Let your images evolve organically with just the right amount of tweaking.

5. Be wary of imagery overkill. Too many, or over-written, images can be tedious if not mind-numbing. When asked how many images a mid-sized poem should contain, my answer is always the same: If you look at the poem you're writing and only find five great lines, then the poem should only be five lines long; in the same way, if you look at a poem you're working on and only find a single brilliant image, then the poem should only contain a single image. And this in closing: Sometimes we write images we love but which aren't quite right for the poem in which we've placed them. When this happens, be prepared to sacrifice an image you love for the sake of the poem. The poem (and your readers) will be grateful.

Poem and Prompt

Love

We lie on warm rocks and watch helicopters
swing down to the river and inhale water.
It's seeing this with you
against the image of last night: the fire
jumping the ridge, its sharp leaps of breath, the trees
that burst into silhouette as we moved
our binoculars to scan the hill for houselights,
the quiet thrill that we could see
these houses burn, watch the fire come down
and hit the water.

—Bronwen Butter Newcott

Newcott takes a risk by titling her poem with an abstract noun, especially one that is so frequently used. We're told to avoid abstracts in poetry, but the poet makes it work by the specificity of her images in the poem. Notice how the initial image leads backward to another one, to *the image of last night*. That second image is the one that gets developed. Notice also the strategic use of the colon that is followed by a catalog of images. Think about how all these images, the ones before and after the colon, are connected to love.

Title your new poem with an abstract word that names an emotion, e.g., hate, jealousy, desire, grief, anger, fear.

Then, using the same structural pattern, write a ten-line poem, or thereabouts, in which you let your images convey the emotion.

Avoid the inclination to tell a story. Let the images do the work.

115

Sample Poems

Passion

Sitting in Adirondack chairs
on the deck,
we watch the sun sink
behind distant trees,
the horizon a brushstroke of deep red,
our fingers entwined,
as the first chill of evening
dances on the breeze.

—Thomas Moudry

After Love

I don't know where my body ends
and yours begins—whose stomach
rumbles. Two become one—like
the Monterey Jack I melted

on crackers for our chilled
Pinot Grigio—not easy to separate—
like fifty years together.
It's silent. No phone or clock. No

outside sounds of jet or truck—
knocks on the door—Parcel Post
or FedEx delivering a package.
You're on your back, holding me.

I'm on my left side, right leg
bent, resting on your thighs,
right hand on your heart.
I doze off to the pulse of the heat

coming on, water rushing through
pipes—glad to lose thoughts
of the day that will come and go,
taking one of us with it.

You stir, as though entering
my mind, but no. I wake to your
weight—the stillness broken only
by the sound of our breathing.

                —Wanda Praisner

Craft Tip #14: What a Figure Can Do

—Susan Laughter Meyers

Even for the plainspoken poet, literal language is not always enough. The just-right use of the figurative—moving beyond the dictionary meaning of words—can open a poem to both broader interpretation and greater exactness. Metaphor and simile are what we first think of when we consider figurative language, but there are enough other rhetorical figures to boggle the mind. And they each serve varying purposes. Apostrophe, personification, hyperbole, metonymy, synecdoche, and oxymoron are just a few. Here are some of the ways they prove useful:

- To use **Apostrophe**, as John Donne does, for example, in *Oh, Death, be not proud*, is to bring to the subject an immediacy not otherwise possible. Direct address can also heighten the emotional appeal, especially when addressing someone who is absent.

- **Personification** creates a similar effect of immediacy. It can enliven a poem and heighten its emotion, as Philip Levine does in "Animals Are Passing from Our Lives," a poem in which the pig speaking is given human qualities: *It's wonderful how I jog / on four honed-down ivory toes.* Personification can be tricky; the key is knowing when to use it and how much is enough in a poem.

- Frost, in "After Apple-Picking," finds a surprisingly convincing way to get across the idea *I have had too much / Of apple picking* with this **Hyperbole**: *There were ten thousand thousand fruit to touch.*

- **Metonymy**, with its substitution of an associated word for the intended one, shortwires the way we think of the substituted term and thereby offers an efficiency of language. In "How She Described Her Ex-Husband When the Police Called," poet Martha Clarkson ends with these

118

lines: *He's the joker pinned in bicycle spokes / vanishing down the street.* Because it's common knowledge that a joker is a playing card, the substitution works.

- **Synecdoche**, with its substitution of a part for the whole, is a type of metonymy, providing that same efficiency. T. S. Eliot uses synecdoche in "The Love Song of J. Alfred Prufrock" in the lines *I should have been a pair of ragged claws / Scuttling across the floors of silent seas.* In doing so, he gives us *claws* as an intentional disembodiment.

- By butting two or more contradictory terms against each other, an **Oxymoron** produces irony and tension, as Shakespeare does with *O brawling love, O loving hate* in *Romeo and Juliet.*

Regardless of which specific figure of speech you use, the effect on the poem is significant and manifold. Partly because of that, it's crucial to beware of overusing figurative language or of using it in a flowery, ornamental way. When called upon to serve the poem, figurative language does more than carry its weight. It can offer a way to say the unsayable. Here are ways your poems can benefit:

- Figures, as Frost called them, increase the musicality of a poem. With prose at one end of the musical range and song at the other, figures of speech move the language toward song. Thus, the use of the figurative can be a tool for lifting a poem that is leaning too far toward the prosaic.

- Figurative language expands a poem's realm of the imaginative. To move beyond the literal is to move into the imaginative. In revision, a good strategy for rescuing a poem that suffers from a failure of the imagination is to turn to figurative language.

- In moving beyond the literal, figurative language contributes to a poem's mystery and surprise.

- A skilled use of figures can go a long way to help make the familiar strange in a poem.

Poem and Prompt

Will

for D'Arcy and Django

My breath, mysterious to me
The long weathers of my arms
My eyes flecked like broken leaves
The crook of my elbow The secret
field under the curve of my hair:

All to be divided between you
so that when you who came from
my body start down our road
when the air is heavy and the frogs
are singing from the swamp
because it has rained or is about
to rain, I will be there.

But in the end—and you cannot
help this, every generation does
the same—you will drive me out.

I will be a rustle in the trees then
as if something had just flown. I
will be the skin that stills the standing
water. And when dusk falls, I will be
a single firefly, blinking green. For I can
never stop being amazed at your beauty,
my music-limbed boy, my woman who
loves numbers in her soul. But wait.
My love for you is hundreds of lanterns
searching the dark. In the gathering night,
look around. I will be all the fireflies.

—Lola Haskins

I admire this poem for its warm expression of love from a mother to her children, a topic that might easily descend into sentimentality but doesn't in this poet's hands. Haskins avoids the sentimental trap via the freshness of her language and figures. Speaking directly to her children, she uses both metaphor and hyperbole, the traditional figures of a love poem.

Notice the setting in the background—rain, trees, dusk, and a road. Notice how the poet draws from that setting for her figures, e.g., *the air is heavy and the frogs / are singing from the swamp,* and one day the mother *will be a rustle in the trees...* But notice, too, the emphasis on numbers that runs throughout the poem. One mother produces two children and divides her attributes (listed in stanza 1) between them. The daughter loves numbers. The mother's love for her children is *hundreds of lanterns.* From single firefly she expands to *all* the fireflies. How nicely the poet combines this numbers motif with hyperbole.

Your challenge is to write a love poem but not to a lover. First, select the person for whom you will write the poem. Perhaps a parent or grandparent, a friend, a teacher, someone who helped you when you needed help, a movie star or someone else you've never met. Perhaps the object of your love need not be human.

Remember or imagine a setting. Brainstorm a list of details from that setting.

Select a minor motif to use throughout your poem. Instead of numbers, you might use references to music, food, tools, flowers, trees.

Now begin to draft your poem. Use Direct Address. Doing so will alter the tone of your poem and move it beyond mere description and declaration. The poem will become intimate and will pull the reader closer.

As you draft your poem, weave in some of the details from your setting.

Incorporate your minor motif.

Work in some metaphors.

Work in some hyperbole, but keep it subtle. If you get too flam-boyant, you will end up with slapstick.

Sample Poems

My Father the Poet

Dad, you climbed my icy roof one January
to redirect a TV antenna.

You taught me how to fix a pipe
that had burst into a forlorn song
of sobbing late one night

and how to open my locked front door
without keys one Christmas Eve
when no locksmith on the planet
would answer the phone.

But Dad, when you read my first book
and asked if I would teach you how
to write a poem,

I froze. Dad, it just happens.
It's like a newspaper hitting
your front door,

a big thump that makes you want to open up.
There isn't a manual that can show
how to put one together ...

You looked puzzled. *I want to write
something for your mother,*
you mumbled sheepishly.

You had never asked for help.
You had never written a poem,
just as I had once never hammered

a dock together. *Don't worry,*
you said, *I bought paper*
and there's a typewriter
in the den.

—Bob Bradshaw

To the Inarticulate Man Who Tries

When you sat in our parlor, originally Nana's,
fire in the fireplace, grandfather clock tocking
contralto, sharing your dreams for all that is
clean and involves the underdog's triumph, I saw

something slack and sensuous around the mouth,
plus that nose straighter than mine, and wanted.
You mentioned how the censors forbade you
to sing, *You'd be ... so sweet to waken with,*

so nice to sit down to eggs and bacon with.
You don't act, you react, you said. I'm that
small-town girl born to dance. Why didn't I
give you anything to react to, just touch

that navy blue and gold tie, just to smooth it,
once? I should have asked, what happens
when your stunt pilot dies, what did the letter
say, that your father gave you before the war,

the one you carried three years? Mother came
downstairs; you had to be going. After the thin man
left, the man who knew too much, the rare breed,
I poked at the fire, a woman who'd said too little.

—Tina Kelley

Craft Tip #15: Metaphor: What Is It Like?

—Ellen Bass

Poetry is rooted in metaphor; things which are superficially different are revealed as being, in some essential way, similar. We say, *This is like that*. And when it's true, when it's accurate, barriers collapse and we get a glimpse into the oneness of the world. But, of course, it's necessary for the metaphor to be vital enough, original enough, to actually do its work.

One of the main functions of metaphor is to heighten emotion. But the more sophisticated we get about language, the less we are moved by its conventional expression. Because of this, we constantly seek ways to make emotion fresh.

So how do we discover the metaphors that will allow us to say the unsayable, to join intimately with the reader? Whether you're writing a first draft or working to revise, here are some practical ideas for opening up the world of metaphor in your poems:

1. *Look in unfamiliar places.*

Many of us operate in metaphoric ruts. Thus, we wind up with an overabundance of similar, overused images. I call this *the green vine school of poetry*. I struggled with this myself for a while, winding up with a glut of garden imagery. If you seem always to be comparing things within some overly familiar territory, look elsewhere. Look under the hood of your car, in your elementary school, in a shoe factory, in a hospital, in the grocery store.

Also, vary the scale. Look small, under the microscope, one thread in a bolt of cloth or even one fiber of the thread. Look big, out into space, back in time to when the stars were born. Getting away from the middle ground can open up a wealth of unexpected images.

126

It's good to look in your imagination, but you can also look literally. If you're trying to think of a metaphor for what it's like to touch your lover's skin, or the pain of cancer, or your dog's exuberance, take that unsolved metaphor with you and look for possibilities throughout your day. As you drive around town, brush your teeth, fold laundry, pay bills, count out change for a customer, look for what your lover's skin might be like. With everything you see or touch or smell, ask yourself, *Is it like this?*

2. *Make lists.*

It can be useful to make lists of metaphors. Write twenty or thirty possible metaphors for what it feels like when your child has a fever or the way dirt clings to a carrot when you pull one out of the ground. It's easier to brainstorm a whole page of ideas that don't have to be good than it is to have to write one perfect metaphor. If you make a list of all the metaphors you can think of (and some can be terrible), you'll loosen up your mind and you may, in the process, stumble upon one that's accurate.

3. *Imitate the holiday ham.*

If you can think in metaphor from the start, that's best, of course. A poem that doesn't have some muscular language working right from the beginning is going to be harder to bring to fruition than one that does. But sometimes we don't have the ability or the good fortune to get those necessary metaphors in the first draft. In that case, it's often possible to go back and add them in. I think of this as the holiday ham method. When you bake a ham, you make little cuts in it and then you stick cloves into the little cuts. That's what you do with the metaphors—you look for places in the poem where you can insert them. For example, you may have a line that says, *She walked toward me.* So you can make a little slit right there and ask yourself, *How did she walk toward me? She walked toward me like ...*

4. *Court strangeness.*

Don't be afraid of the strange. Galway Kinnell said, *It's okay to have something strange in your poem. In fact, it's preferable.* Strangeness is often where the most interesting images live. Be willing to be wild, to go out on a limb, to risk making a fool of yourself. If you always stay safe with your metaphors, you'll miss out on too much. You'll be censoring your metaphors before you even generate them. Often metaphors which seem too odd when you write them turn out to be the most resonant.

Ultimately, the metaphors need to deepen the impact of your poem or they'll detract from it. Beautiful or interesting or wonderfully strange as they might be, every metaphor must be in service to the poem. Anything that doesn't enhance the poem diminishes it. But it's easier to take out a metaphor that's not needed than to write a brilliant metaphor. So while you're in the generative mode, don't be overly critical. You may put a dozen metaphors in your poem and only wind up using one, but if it's the right one, that's all you need.

Poem and Prompt

I Recant, Vol. II

I'm not a silkworm. I'm not a walnut
soaked in wine, not an almond in Cointreau.
I am not thought vast within a pillow,
not a labyrinth, not an odd inkblot.
I have not roused an old souse from her rut,
have not started a riot in Cairo,
have stirred no deep, deliquescent sorrow.
I have caused no argument in Zagat.
I am unaddressed in the best cafes
where I am lesser thumb, a background cough,
underpaid, scant hoodoo, verminous fluff.
Among proffered options I am unweighed,
in multiple choice, when compared to you,
oozy rat in a sanitary zoo.

—Hailey Leithauser

So much negativity here. I like the layer of complication that adds to the poem. Leithauser makes a catalog of all that her speaker is *not*. From this series of negative metaphors, we must then figure out what the speaker *is*. The next thing that catches my attention is the playfulness. Of course, she's not a walnut or an almond!

The form of this poem calls for our attention. It's a sonnet, each line with ten syllables. The diction is also very appealing. Leithauser doesn't settle for easy words but goes for ones like *Cointreau, labyrinth, inkblot, souse, deliquescent, verminous.*

129

Your challenge is to write your own sonnet. Think of a topic that's phrased as a negative—where you have not lived, what you don't want, men or women you have not loved, what you won't give up.

Now brainstorm a snazzy list of negative statements. Don't worry about whether or not they go together.

Draft your list into a poem, making a catalog of the statements. Use some of the anaphora (repetition of beginning words) that Leithauser has used—*I am not, I have not, I am*. This device adds music.

Can you switch it up a bit in the last six lines? Move from the *not* metaphors to positive ones beginning with *I am*—though these are hardly positive in Leithauser's poem (*I am lesser thumb, a background cough...*).

Intensify your diction.

See if you can duplicate the rhyme scheme used here: abba abba cddc ee.

Aim for ten syllables per line. Go for the music.

Mega challenge: Has anyone been clever enough to figure out that the last line is a palindrome? Leithauser has written a series of poems, each of which contains a palindrome. Here are three she wrote but never used. Can you work one of them into your poem? Or create your own?

1. erase sorrow or roses are

2. In it, ram a martini

3. O, I'd a rapid dip, a radio

Sample Poems

You might suspect

I'm not immortal, not a humongous
fungus, tossing spores, spreading underground,
not tenacious as barnacles around
rocks and ships' hulls, not pure beef from Angus
cattle. You thought I hid lines and wrinkles
with silicone and Botox? I simply
let my genes determine what I will be
with age. Who cares if some men don't twinkle
at my sight. When you look closely, you'll see
watercolors and felt-tips I've hoarded,
batiks and velveteens for your envy.
These frayed and frumpy clothes are not sordid.
As an artist, I'm fated to be weird,
in sloppy decadence my parents feared.

—Joan Mazza

Gassing Up in New Jersey, Just before Midnight

I'm not the nude pin-up in your back room—
nothing but a garter, lipstick, and smile.
I'm not caressing my stick to beguile,
nor am I here for a little *vroom vroom*.
I didn't go empty so you can loom
waist level by my cracked window awhile
nor to excite you because I'm hostile
and hate your nozzle and your hose and fume.
I am here to stare your hand off my trunk,
to blast you Gielgud reciting Shakespeare,
to not look to my mirror where you leer,
to tell myself you're lonely and you're drunk.
And I'm glad I wasn't born a weenie.
Fill *your* tank—in it, ram a martini.

—Susanna Rich

The Poet on the Poem: Cecilia Woloch

Blazon

after Breton

My love with his hair of nightingales
With his chest of pigeon flutter, of gray doves preening themselves
         at dawn
With his shoulders of tender balconies half in shadow, half in sun
My love with his long-boned thighs the map of Paris of my tongue
With his ink-stained tongue, his tongue the tip
of a steeple plunged into milky sky
My love with his wishing teeth
With his fingers of nervous whispering, his fingers of a boy
whose toys were cheap and broken easily
My love with his silent thumbs
With his eyes of a window smudged of a train that passes in the night
With his nape of an empty rain coat
hung by the collar, sweetly bowed
My love with his laughter of an empty stairwell, rain all afternoon
With his mouth the deepest flower to which
I have ever put my mouth

DL: I like the simplicity of your title. How did you arrive at "Blazon"?

CW: This question makes me smile, because I think that I'm very bad at titles and therefore I always just go for the simplest, most obvious and least potentially embarrassing thing. So a lot of my poems have one-word titles, as do all of my books. I always write something at the top of the page when I start to write, and I put that in parentheses, as a kind of working title, and usually I end up just taking the parentheses away and making that the title. So, in some way, the poem comes with its title—maybe the working title is my semi-conscious *intent* when I begin to write, and thus the most apt thing, after all?

In this case, I wrote "blazon" at the top of the page because I'd given myself an exercise that I'd given to the writers in my Paris Poetry Workshop, and I usually try to do the exercises I assign. So I'd assigned a blazon—a poem of praise for a beloved, from the French tradition, which is a kind of catalog or list poem enumerating the physical attributes of the beloved and using a metaphor to describe each of those attributes. The poem I used as a model was André Breton's blazon, "Free Union," which is full of astounding metaphors like *My woman with her shoulders of champagne.* I stole Breton's anaphora and substituted *my love* for *ma femme*, and also used *with* to begin some lines, as Breton does. Then I worked from a list of images I'd compiled, mixing them up in different ways and applying them to particular physical attributes of a particular beloved. So the poem evolved from the title, which was the exercise, and since I couldn't come up with another title after the poem was finished, I left it at that.

DL: I'm intrigued by your use of punctuation in this poem. You use no periods and commas only internally. Tell us why.

CW: I went back and forth about this, as I'm notoriously particular about grammar and punctuation. But I felt that, since the anaphora came at the beginning of each line on the page, punctuation wasn't necessary and seemed to just get in the way of the flow of the poem. I capitalized the first word of each line that begins with the anaphora, and that seemed enough to indicate to the reader that a new item was being added to the list.

DL: This poem is structured by anaphora. Lines beginning with *My love* alternate with lines beginning with *With his*. Although the lines appear to have spontaneously tumbled out in their current order, I suspect that they didn't. When in your drafting did the anaphora come in? How much rearranging of lines did you do?

CW: The first draft of any poem is always fairly spontaneous, for me; but I did a lot of rearranging, in this case. Lines tumbled out and tumbled around, and other lines came tumbling in and changed the sequence, and other lines ended up being left out because they didn't fit in the sequence, ultimately, or because they didn't seem fresh to me. It's hard to write love poems because the tendency is to swoon, and it's hard to swoon in an original way. So I took my time with this poem; I wasn't in a hurry to finish it. I'd put it away for long periods of time and then come back to it and fiddle around with the metaphors and the sequence. I'm not convinced that I didn't leave out some good things, some of my favorite lines, but you reach a point at which it's time to leave the poem alone. The anaphora was there from the beginning—or rather, both of them were. I fiddled around with how often each anaphora was repeated, because I wanted the rhythm of repetition, but wanted to vary it, too.

DL: You employ a catalog in this poem and in others. What draws you to the catalog and how do you generate it?

CW: I've read that the catalog, or list, is the oldest form of poetry, and that our earliest written documents are lists and catalogs. So maybe it's the most *natural* form of writing? To be honest, I write lists when I can't think of any other way to begin. I like the freedom that the catalog gives us to leap from one thing to another, to work by association and subvert our tendency to try to be rational and linear. And I always want to begin writing in a state of unknowing, a state of bewilderment, so that I can let the language itself lead me to some revelation, some discovery, something I hadn't known I knew or thought or felt. And using an anaphora, a repeated word or phrase at the beginning of each line, provides a kind of rhythm, and rhythm can become incantatory, and incantation leads us into another state of mind and being, a state of en-chant-ment, and thus allows for the possibility of magic. I'm always after magic, in poetry, and in love, too, I suppose.

DL: This lovely poem is richly laced with metaphors. Tell us about *hair of nightingales, his ink-stained tongue,* and the

135

stunning *his mouth the deepest flower to which / I have ever put my mouth.*

CW: Again, I was doing the exercise I'd assigned to my students in Paris, and the first step of the exercise was to gather a list of images from our surroundings, and then to gather a list of imagery associated with a particular beloved, and then to experiment with mixing them up. So the pigeons and balconies and sky and stairwell and rain and such were gathered from what I was seeing around me in Paris; the hair of nightingales and the ink-stained tongue and the deepest flower of that mouth were things that came to mind when I thought about the physical being of this dark and mysterious and very particular beloved. I think to write an honest and original love poem, it's best to try to be as specific as possible, while allowing the mystery of the *other* into the chemistry of the poem—not vagueness, but mystery.

Bonus Prompt: The Extravagant Love Poem

This prompt will result in a poem of metaphors. Work quickly. Don't overthink what you're doing. Let the metaphors leap.

Begin your first line with "You are my _____."

Now complete the first line with #1 from the numbered list of categories below.

Then leave some open space and proceed to #2 and so on.

(Remember to begin each line with the same opening phrase and to leave open space between lines.)

1. a dessert (e.g., crème brûlée)

2. a beverage

3. a bird

4. a jewel

5. a tree

6. a flower

7. a body of water

8. something from a category of your own choosing

Go back now and add details in the open spaces, e.g., line 1 might become: *You are my crème brûlée, my jiggly pudding, the hint of caramel in my mouth.*

Finish your draft by repeating line 1 as your closing line.

Rearrange the order of the lines if you like.

Consider changing from present to past tense. This adjustment will be a dramatic eye opener as time and tone completely shift. New possibilities will open up.

You may like the neatness of the circular structure; or you might like the impact of another startling closing metaphor. Feel free to eliminate the repeated metaphor.

Polish the language. This poem is a lyric; it should sing.

A variation of this prompt:

Repeat the same activity, but now create metaphors that express anger and unhappiness, e.g., *You were the soufflé that wouldn't rise*. If you want variety, you can change the categories.

VI. Going Deep / Adding Layers

Follow your inner moonlight; don't hide the madness.

—Allen Ginsberg

Craft Tip #16: Drawing Blood: How to Go Deep

—Jan Beatty

*Poems are like dreams, in them you put what you don't
know you know.*
    —Adrienne Rich

*Rationality squeezes out much that is rich and juicy and
fascinating.*
    —Anne Lamott

As writers, we want to explore the idea of blood as the highway of the body, the red road that carries our unspoken dreams, our network of pleasure, the unarticulated bridges between us, our tunnel of redemption. But how do we find the *blood* in our poems, the red road that carries these unspoken dreams? How do we avoid the distant, ill-defined, vague writing that doesn't engage? How do we find the bridges to the fire beneath the lines?

Consider this short poem by James Allen Hall:

Family Portrait

When I say my mother, the thing inside me
that strips for you begins to writhe
under burlesque lighting, leaves a sweat outline in your sheets.

When I say my father, the taunting auctioneer
comes forward and bows at the waist, smiling.
When I say my father, he hands me the camera,

he says, Go ahead, big shot, take her picture.
So I do, I maul her into memory.

When I say the end, no embrace, no vengeance
can bring her back. When I say I loved her,

I mean no story is true.
Not even tenderness lasts.

This poem transports us inside through the elements of mystery and surprise. We are not expecting a poem entitled "Family Portrait" to begin with stripping and burlesque. The voice in this poem keeps us steadily invested. We don't know where it's going, yet we are never confused. We feel a sense of intimate telling, as if this is a hard-won truth that is being divulged. This feeling is set up through the image of writhing and sweat—whatever is being related is not a minor thing.

The leaping from stanza to stanza supports the leaping of content, and slows the poem, supporting the continued mystery. Yet, when we arrive at the last stanza, we are told: ... *no story is true*. We are kept off balance. There is no comfortable resolution for the reader, which mirrors the content of the poem.

It's essential for us, as writers, to write what we're afraid to write—the very thing we sometimes try to avoid saying. That writing will stretch us so that we can encounter the sweet deep inside of the body that runs us tight like a clock and wild like an animal, but always moving along the line of uncertainty.

As Jane Hirshfield has said, *Originality does demand courage, the courage to become a person who is able to know his or her experience deeply, who is willing to feel and to question feeling, to dig for what the truth of a moment is, including the truth that may contradict external fact.*

Poem and Prompt

I Held the Axe,

knowing it's not
the right tool against
the tulips, the wild blooming
field. But still ...
still loving its heft.

The blue morpho lowers a wing;
the sky comes down. I could
wound what's wounded me;
that blade keeps its blaze. I'm the lengths
it would go, the aim of effort
in a tight little palm of promise.

To stay those blooms.
Tulips' petals of tears
in the mind. Or to stand—
a minute? a lifetime?—
as a threat until the threat's
passed. To stand among these
sweet young grasses
just beginning to sprout
over the trouble
and through the heart.

—Nance Van Winckel

The mystery in this poem immediately appealed to me. I'm not
quite sure what's going on. Why would the speaker want to
attack the tulips and why would she knowingly choose the
wrong tool? How has the speaker been wounded? By the tulips?
Should she kill them or let them stand? There's ambiguity here,

the kind of ambiguity that some of us deliberately weed out of our poems fearing no one will *get* them. For this new poem, let's not go in fear of ambiguity. Let's not be overly attracted to clarity.

First, choose an instrument. A different kind of tool, such as a hammer, adz, awl, chainsaw. Or perhaps a pair of scissors, a flashlight, a rope, a ladder, a spatula. Take the instrument somewhere to do a job for which it is not intended or suited.

Use first person. Let your title be the first part of the first sentence. Let it run into the first line. Just let the writing flow out of you.

Think about destroying something and bring this into your draft. Let something beautiful enter the scene.

Raise a few questions. Leave them unanswered. Use some incomplete sentences.

Divide your first draft into at least three stanzas.

Go back through your draft, adding, deleting, moving around. Make the poem your own. Feel free to change any of the directions in order to do that. You might switch to third person. Or plural.

Notice that Van Winckel's first stanza is past tense; the second switches to present. Try that risky shift. Then feel free to abandon it.

Do you need more than three stanzas? Van Winckel uses short lines. If you begin with short lines, perhaps you'll later want to experiment with longer ones.

Sample Poems

Here I am

weed-whacking with a spatula
flipping hash browns with an Emory board
filing my nails with a knife

Suddenly I know precisely
what to do with these tears
though look already they're smoldering

Here I am
hedge clipping
the wine-stained flutes

shard-scatter like a flock
of merlin-shocked sanderlings
With a needle I'm digging up

the something stupid I said
to the sand crabs
to the rising tide

Here I am
with the spoke before I thought
with the sizzling sea

with this most unhelpful implement

—Martha Silano

Your Grandmother's Whisk

is not round but curves in a half-circle,
its wire hand flashing silver as I whip
my breakfast eggs into foam.

I curl my palm around the worn
wooden handle, smoothed to a soft
patina by her grip and yours, wonder

what ghosts linger even now in her
lost kitchen, waiting to be fed.
She had chickens, gathered fresh eggs

to break on the lip of some pottery bowl,
whisked them into buttermilk, flour, and
baking powder, maybe making a batter

for those blueberry pancakes you loved.
Perhaps she baked a cake to honor your birth,
my love, now more than seventy years ago.

Would I could whisk you both back into
my kitchen, offer you some still warm
scrambled eggs this winter dawn.

—Penny Harter

146

Craft Tip #17: Contraries

—Gray Jacobik

I find myself cringing at poetry readings when the poet apologizes because he or she is about to read a *dark* poem, and likewise, when the word is *now for something on the lighter side*. My inner voice is shouting: *Give me light AND dark!* History moves by *contraries* William Butler Yeats believed, and so, too, do good poems. Yeats put into practice the great grace of rocking the poem through contraries, or opposites, making sure a noble act was paired with a despicable one, day with night, interior with exterior, the sacred with the profane, the objective with the subjective, and so on. Pairings, pairings, pairings: we love poems that take us through these motions. Here's a little one by Yeats to show you what I mean:

He Wishes For the Cloths of Heaven

Had I the heavens' embroidered cloths,
Enwrought with golden and silver light,
The blue and the dim and the dark cloths
Of night and light and the half light,
I would spread the cloths under your feet:
But I, being poor, have only my dreams;
I have spread my dreams under your feet;
Tread softly because you tread on my dreams.

We see contraries at work most obviously in lines 3 and 4 where the *blue and the dim* and the *dark cloths / Of night and light and the half light* contrast so beautifully with the *golden and silver light* of line 2, but there are larger movements of contraries as well. The speaker is saying to his beloved that had he all the wealth of heaven he would give it to her, but since he's poor he can give her only his dreams. *I would spread the cloths under your feet*, a lavish gesture for someone who is dispossessed of material wealth, but one that speaks to the magnitude of the speaker's love.

So there are the larger contraries of material/immaterial, rich/poor, having/not-having, although ironically, *the heavens' embroidered cloths*—a metaphor for the beauty of the skies whatever the hour—are themselves immaterial and available to all. One more contrary I see: the poem ends with a request, *Tread softly*; however, up to that point, the rhetorical strategy has been that of using the suppositional (*Had I ... I would spread ...*), then the simple declarative (*I have spread ...*). Yeats takes a last turn and ends in the imperative voice, making the request a directive.

In this poem, we have the contraries of light and dark, rich and poor, give and take, wedded to the poet's advancing the action through shifts in voice from the suppositional to the declarative to the imperative.

When you're working through your draft revisions, consider the question, *How can I add an opposite or contrary energy?* If the poem is humorous, add some gravity. If it is a rapturous romp, stir in some somber thoughts and imagery. If yours is a *dark* poem, turn the speaker's thoughts and perceptions toward the opposite pole on the emotional spectrum. You don't have to be as obvious as stating *hot/cold, day/night, up/down, inside/outside, self/other*. Instead, go hunting for metaphors, implied or directly stated, and for other figurations and imagery that can bring a contrary (or two!) into play. Irony is, of course, whether verbal or dramatic, inherently contradictory, as are hyperbole and understatement.

A shift in diction toward words that carry opposite connotations is another way to work some contraries into your evolving text. You open the poem, expand its scope, by including contraries, and, as a bonus, the poem becomes more credible, more grounded in reality, for as we all know (and remember this comes from a woman named *Gray*)—nothing's all black or white.

Poem and Prompt

In Answer to Amy's Question What's a Pickerel

Pickerel have infinite, small bones, and skins
of glass and black ground glass, and though small for pike
are no less wall-eyed and their eyes like bone.
Are fierce for their size, and when they flare
at the surface resemble drowning birds,
the wing-slick panic of birds, but in those
seconds out of water on the line,
when their color changes and they choose for life,
will try to cut you and take part of your hand
back with them. And yet they open like hands,
the sweet white meat more delicate in oil,
to be eaten off the fire when the sun
is level with the lake, the wind calm,
the air ice-blue, blue-black, and flecked with rain.

—Stanley Plumly

The poet begins with a simple question, presumably asked by a child, and then proceeds to build the poem one image after another in such a way that the response is anything but simple and childlike. Notice how Plumly alternates fierce, frightening images with delicate, lovely ones.

Read this poem aloud. Notice its music. Notice that most lines have eleven syllables. Notice the strong beats and the use of monosyllabic words. Notice the strong syllable that ends each line. As you read aloud, you can hear the effect of these devices.

For your own poem begin with a question. What's a raccoon? A conch shell? A sausage? A portobello? Spanish moss? Let the question serve as your title.

Brainstorm a bunch of images.

Then do a bit of research and add to the list of images. Draft the poem. As you move through your drafts and polish the poem, think about your word choices. Choose words that enhance your images and create music.

You might want to strive for something sonnet-like with the 14 lines that Plumly uses and his close to ten-syllable lines.

Sample Poems

Anatomy Lesson

The heart is veined like a carnelian agate,
red on deeper red, dusky pink on purple,

and though it governs your life-blood
it's not much larger than your fist.

It pumps like a fist impassioned, its cadence
shock after shock it jumps at, forcing

the blood through arteries curled
like a nest of baby mice inside you.

They go wherever you go, blind channellers.
The heart only vaguely resembles the heart

you learned in preschool, construction
paper red, the one you learned to cross

and hope to die, the one you use to signal
love. Now you try hard to have your heart

in the right place. You've learned not
to wear it on your sleeve or lose it

at the first sign of discouragement.
It throbs for its own reasons, throbs

even when broken, just beats harder.

—Lisken Van Pelt Dus

Flood Washed

On the asphalt lies a question mark
two feet long—

brown mosaic triangles, beige stripes,
narrow head.

With reluctant thumb and forefinger
I spin it

over, belly down. A fatal slit
down the side.

Bird's beak, perhaps. If alive, just
its sliding

stir would have chilled to shiver.
Pity now,

and curiosity. Pretty—
so pretty—

how could Eve—or I—not be lured?
Glossy coat,

graceful neck. *Snake!* our children
in terror,

had raced from the backyard bushes.
Young husband-

father dug his hoe, down and down.
Conqueror,

protector of household and clan
from beauty.

Who framed you, the visionary
poet asks—

from whence comes this earthly design
built into

matter's insistent desire: In
all things, form.

—Charlotte Mandel

Craft Tip #18: Confronting Your Fears

—Alicia Ostriker

A line that is always present at the back of my poetry-mind is the closing line of Muriel Rukeyser's "Double Ode": *Do I move toward form, do I use all my fears?*

You might think this line is a tangle of contradictions. Isn't *form* in poetry, as in life, a matter of control, a matter of order? And aren't emotions, including our fears, just the opposite of controlled and orderly? And aren't emotions something you either conquer or surrender to? That's just the point, isn't it? Poems are contradictions. Or impossibilities. But the impossible has happened before and may happen again, at any time. You read the line, *Do I move toward form, do I use all my fears*, and you intuitively know what Rukeyser means. So when you write, you reach for the place where the inner and the outer fuse—where emotion is captured (not just named) by words and phrases with their sounds and cadences and the way they relate to the time and space around them.

The idea that poets neither conquer nor surrender to their fears, but use them, and find form through them—to me, that is brilliant. Because fears—notice the plural—are part of our deepest selves. We have fears from the time we are born. Rukeyser wrote this as an aging woman, so fear of death must be part of what this poem points to, but the poem also evokes mother and father—as symbols, as realities, as dreams of *old gifts and wars*. She tells herself, *Pay attention to what they tell you to forget*. This can be difficult, because we have to un-censor ourselves. In a poem of mine I describe the poet as fishing waist-deep in a stream:

> jigs of splashy light teasing the eye
> delighting not distracting you
>
> from the thing you are trying to catch
> that is trying to flee

And a mantra in my writing workshops is *Write what you are afraid to write*. It is a lifelong task. Use the fears. Bring them up from the subconscious, and find the words, find the form. People will thank you, because your deep truth will speak to their own mute depths. Get out of the closet. There's another poem of Rukeyser's that reminds us of how much we share as human beings, literally under the surface:

Isands

> Oh for God's sake
> they are connected
> underneath

How to go fishing for the truth within you that is hiding or *trying to flee*? Try these methods:

1. When someone else's poem strikes you as brave, choose a word or image from that poem and start riffing on it.

2. When a memory of keen suffering or keen delight rises in your mind, picture the scene—go for the images.

3. When you hear the inner censor warning, *Don't say that*— catch the moment, and start saying it.

4. When you find yourself explaining or commenting, stop. Go back to the images.

Poem and Prompt

White Towels

I have been studying the difference
between solitude and loneliness,
telling the story of my life
to the clean white towels taken warm from the dryer.
I carry them through the house
as though they were my children
asleep in my arms.

—Richard Jones

In spite of its mere seven lines, there's quite a bit going on in this poem. Notice that the poem begins with the speaker considering the distinction between two words which might be considered synonyms but aren't. Not quite. There's some essential difference.

Then notice that the speaker is talking to an object, something that can't respond to the telling of his story. And don't you wonder what that story might be? But the poet doesn't tell us. Or does he? Is there perhaps a hint in the simile that closes the poem? Finally, notice syntax. The poem is just two sentences, each beginning with *I* and followed by a verb.

Your first challenge is to find a pair of closely related words. Some possible pairings: castle and palace, despair and sorrow, love and adore, creek and brook.

Meditate on your two words and see where they lead you. Hit the dictionary.

Begin your draft, first person, present time. Get an object in there. Let it evolve into simile. What else could your object be? What is it like?

Feeling contrary? Some possible variations: girl and tree, guilt and quilt, sweetbreads and sweet breads, bring and take.

This might be hard. All the better and the deeper the reward.

Sample Poems

Grief Beyond Sorrow

The fishing lure cast by my father
slicing the surface of the Tennessee River,
his hammer pounding the boat dock,
I hear. I hear blues, Muddy Waters on the radio,
on a Sunday family excursion to Shiloh,
battleground with blood under the green.
Listen—hear the oars of the long boat,
the shouts of the oarsmen, the helmsman,
come to take my father
across the dark waters.

—Broeck Wahl Blumberg

Sleeveless

I never noticed the difference
between naked and exposed
until your sweater was puddled on my floor
and your shoulders remained covered
in kaleidoscopic swirls of ink. A tattooed
cartography of memories and myths.
Sleeves I could never remove.

—Shawnte Orion

The Poet on the Poem: Patricia Fargnoli

Will the Cows Come Home?

When the river freezes over and the pot boils
When the cat leaves the corner, when the tulips leave the bed

After absence has made your heart grow fonder
After the apples have fallen far from the tree

Where the village is sleeping, the cows will come to the barn
Swishing their long tails, nodding their heads

If you have been waiting too long, the cows will come for you
If you believe in cows, they will come to your hand

If you hold out sweet grass in late afternoon's last hour
From the greener pastures, they will surely come to you

When you say the right sounds, they will hear you
When your house is made of glass and stones, they will see you

When what has gone around must come around
They will come home

Be careful what you wish for; if something can go wrong it will
But where there's a will there's a way

After the cat's nine lives are through and the dog's bone is buried
After the wishbone's been broken and the turkey's been eaten

Go with the flow of the river. The cows will come home
After your actions have spoken louder than words

Before all good things have come to an end
Before all the bridges have burned

The cows will come home

If the rolling stone has gathered its moss and is still
If the salt has been thrown over the barn's shoulder

All things come to those who wait
Cometh the hour, cometh the cows

Better late than never, everything in its own good time
The cows will come home

To your barn shaking their bells
They will come home to you.

DL: What led you to choose cows as a topic for a poem? As the poem progresses, they seem to become more than merely cows. Was that your intention?

PF: I had just been to buy raw milk from a local dairy farm where I'd stood at the fence talking to the Holsteins and loving their broad innocent faces. So I thought why not write another cow poem (I've written a few). And the phrase *when will the cows come home* came into my head. But I haven't a clue where the idea came from to answer the question by playing with sayings. The muse was on the job that day, I guess. But the next thing I did was, with the help of Google, make a long list of popular sayings. Then (and when I had the rhythm) the poem almost wrote itself. Which, I might say, is much different than my usual struggle over months or years process.

And yes, the cows become more than merely cows, though I don't know that I realized that at first. They are, perhaps, whatever we wait for. Though I don't know if that's it exactly either. One of the early lessons I learned when I was learning to write was this: If one writes exactly enough about a specific thing, object, image, or event, sometimes it gathers a deeper meaning (or another level of meaning) beyond that exact description. I think that is true in this case.

DL: You violate one of the first rules taught to novice poets: Avoid clichés. Instead, you embrace them—and to great advantage. What made you decide to take this risk and what do you think makes it work?

PF: I wasn't thinking of these as clichés exactly but mostly as sayings: aphorisms, platitudes, proverbs that have been around for a long time and which have been used as lessons for humans about life. What's changed here, of course, is that I've made them apply to cows—a shift in perspective. Anyway, I love breaking rules in poems and getting away with it. An early poetry teacher, Brendan Galvin, taught me that what works is the only final rule.

DL: Your use of anaphora adds music, structure, and meaning. How hard did you work on that technique? Also, the refrain, *The cows will come home*, or a slight variation, adds such power to the poem. How conscious was this?

PF: It was very conscious. I read somewhere that Stanley Kunitz once said that when he had the rhythm of a beginning poem in his head, the poem could be written. I may be remembering that wrong, but he said something like that and it struck me as being true. And the refrain and anaphora keep the poem focused and glued together. The repetition builds power as it goes, I think.

DL: In the third to last stanza, you say, *Cometh the hour; cometh the cows*. That change in diction immediately grabbed my attention. Why *cometh*?

PF: The proverb I was playing with and paralleling here is *Cometh the hour; cometh the man*. This is my favorite line, precisely because of the surprise of the change in diction—and because of its rhythm.

DL: Tell us why there's no punctuation at line ends.

PF: There's no end punctuation at all except for the final period. That just seemed intuitively right to keep the flow going. I let capital letters and line and stanza breaks substitute for punctuation.

DL: Tell us why each line begins with the formality of a capital letter.

PF: Because I felt that each line was almost an end-stopped sentence—or at least a sentence fragment and I wanted them to be read that way. Again, this was intuitive and seemed right.

Bonus Prompt: The Fusion of Opposites Poem

1. Choose one of the following:

    quiet

    hot

    happy

    near

    bright

    Now imagine a scene or incident that pertains to your choice. Write ten lines about that. Each line should be one sentence.

2. Now take the opposite of your above choice:

    noisy

    cold

    sad

    far

    dark

    Again, imagine a scene or incident that pertains to your concept. On a separate piece of paper, write ten lines about that. Each line should be one sentence.

3. On a new piece of paper, write the first line of the first piece. Follow that with the first line of the second piece. Keep alternating lines until you've used up all twenty lines. For example, a hot line will be followed by a cold one, then a hot

one, and so on. You might want to also try beginning with the second piece instead of the first.

4. Add any fillers you need to achieve clarity, but trust weirdness. Delete what mars the poem.

5. Play with line breaks and stanza form. This might work well as a prose poem.

VII. Syntax

Art washes from the soul the dust of everyday life.

—Pablo Picasso

Craft Tip #19: Fooling with Syntax

—Jeffrey Harrison

With all the attention poets pay to lines and line breaks, we can sometimes lose sight of the importance of sentences and syntax. A wide variety of sentence structures is available to us, and one of the most important formal considerations in writing a poem is the relationship between sentences and lines and the many ways they can interact.

My general suggestion is simply to pay more attention to syntax and all its possibilities as you write poems. Are you relying too much on one kind of sentence, for example, the simple declarative sentence favored in so many first-person, image-based poems? Remember that syntax is related to argument, which is to say to the speaker's stance, and therefore to voice. Modulations in syntax help us enact the drama of a speaker struggling to say something.

Take a look, for instance, at the last two stanzas of Philip Larkin's poem, "Mr Bleaney":

> But if he stood and watched the frigid wind
> Tousling the clouds, lay on the fusty bed
> Telling himself that this was home, and grinned,
> And shivered, without shaking off the dread

> That how we live measures our own nature,
> And at his age having no more to show
> Than one hired box should make him pretty sure
> He warranted no better, I don't know.

The syntax here may seem roundabout and indirect, with all the seemingly hypothetical action displaced into a long series of dependent clauses and the main clause not coming until the end. But the complex syntax mirrors the speaker's complicated feelings about his life—including its possible unimportance—as seen through the lens of the apartment's previous tenant.

I don't mean to imply that complex syntax is always the way to go. Different poems call for different methods, and there are times when the direct approach of a simple declarative works best. The point is to be aware of different syntactic possibilities. If you are stuck in a poem, or if the poem feels inert or just *not right* somehow, take a look at the syntax, starting at the beginning of the poem.

The poem's opening words are, in a sense, the angle of entry into the poem, and you may need to adjust that angle. You might want to ask yourself how you actually feel about the subject matter, and what you are trying to say about it, as a way of finding your opening salvo. Or you might simply experiment with different kinds of first sentences—a periodic sentence, an imperative, a question—and see where that takes you. In the process, you may discover feelings you didn't know you had about the subject. One thing is certain: if you change the syntax of the opening phrasing, everything that follows will also have to change. And the different structure that results may bring the poem together, reorganize it, and make it whole.

Poem and Prompt

Swifts at Evening

The whoosh of rush hour traffic washes through my head
as I cross the bridge through the treetops into my neighborhood
    and what's left of my thoughts is sucked up suddenly
by a huge whirlwind of birds, thousands of chimney swifts
  wheeling crazily overhead against a sky just beginning
      to deepen into evening-turning round and round
        in their erratic spiral ragged at the edges
    where more chittering birds join in the circling
    flock from every direction, having spent all
        day on the wing scattered for miles across
      September skies and now pulled into the
        great vortex that funnels into the air-
          shaft of the library, the whole day
            going like water down a drain with
              the sucking sound of traffic and
                the birds swirling like specks
                  of living sediment drawn from
                  the world into the whirlpool
                    into the word-pool flapping
                      like bats at the last
                        moment diving and
                          turning into
                            words.

—Jeffrey Harrison

What a fabulous, breath-taking, breathless pace this poem has. That's achieved primarily by syntax. Notice that the entire poem is a single sentence.

Notice how the poem brings in metaphors in the last third. That, too, adds to the intensity. And the sounds—*world, whirlpool, word-pool, words*. Notice the predominance of *s* and *w* sounds throughout. Notice the line breaks, how they compel you to move quickly to the next line.

Now pick a topic, something you have seen that merits description—the river cresting, flood waters filling the streets, goldfinches at the feeder, a tree toppling, a deer frozen in the headlights of an oncoming car. Let yourself be distracted by the sight you choose, then completely absorbed by it.

Get your chosen sight into the beginning of your draft and go from there, describing and describing. Write without stopping to think. Just write.

Once you have your draft, rework the poem into one sentence. Plug in some metaphors, especially as the poem builds towards its end.

Which sounds dominate your poem? Choose two or three and exploit them.

Harrison's poem is a concrete poem, that is, it takes the physical shape of its subject. You might want to try this. The risk is the possibility of trivializing your poem.

Sample Poems

Ceremony for the Deer

Lay the deer on the shallow ground
after having carried her for miles,
from under the oak
where she bled,

pray for the dead,
the young dead,
all of them you remember,
their tendrils of hair,
the noise their legs made when they ran,

let the wind waft
the papery leaves,
make more leaves,
make a sound of whispering,

and cover the shallow ground
with white winter grass
and flowers,
the pyrocantha,
the chrysanthemum snow,
new and soft between your hands.

—Linda Benninghoff
published in *Verse Wisconsin*

The Beach House

The tornado churning its wake of white across the flat of ocean,
the clouds, dark, heavy, low, billowing urgent, tracking east,
  the sudden whoosh of wind, deck furniture sliding, crashing,
    glass shattering, the shower of stone cascading overhead,
      tar paper and other pieces of roofing material flying,
      heavy steel door frisbee'd to the beach, the building
      trembling, the man as well thinking of danger, spun
      into the sky, crushed by a falling refrigerator,
or decapitated by a flying cribbage board,
thinking too of a place to hide, like under
 the bed that was too narrow to crawl,
  or the basement we didn't have,
    thinking until   sudden stillness
     stopped thought and quiet
     opened the door for
     curiosity to peer out,
      see the grey vortex,
      that vicious viper
      spin, twirl,
        tail-dance,
         twine,
          and spit
           water.

—John Hutchinson

172

Craft Tip #20: The Promise of Syntax

—JoAnn Balingit

A combination of the Beatles, the bookmobile, and the beautiful task of diagramming sentences in Mrs. Penn's class brought out what would be the poet in me. Mrs. Penn was—as Mark Twain called the pterodactyl—*a mighty starchy critter*. Her severity made kids love to hate eighth-grade English at Southwest Junior High. But in her presence, I got my geek on. Not only for the *Reader's Guide to Periodical Literature* and its miniscule headings, but for dependent and independent clauses and for past perfect and subjunctive, did I fall hard. Mrs. Penn fostered my nascent faith that all things language would be my shelter in the world. I took the stern tone of her English as a sign of reverence.

Pencil in hand at age 13, I felt the promise of syntax—its alchemy, transformation, power—and the endless possibilities of ancient patterns and broken molds.

Syntax refers to word order—the grammar of a sentence, its architecture. Poetry that works outside the boundaries of traditional versification—of meter and rhyme—still has at its disposal, Linda Gregerson points out, *a great formal inheritance*. It has syntax, described by Gregerson as *the vested depository of memory and anticipation; the engine of forward momentum; the thing that ties one word to another, one moment to the one to come.*

Syntax in poetry promises the reader, who obediently holds one thing in mind, that a complimentary thing will arrive. Syntax is the promise that there will be a next thing. And syntax is one tool the poet uses to break the promise, to bait and switch, or to set the reader up in one direction and swerve off into another.

A poet breaks with common syntax to draw attention to what the poem is saying and how it is said. The most common

syntactical move is inverted word order: *Love is not love /
Which alters when it alteration finds.* Shakespeare inverts the
verb and direct object to emphasize the charge. Inversions can
mirror the struggle of confusion—or, paradoxically, the
strength and composure of insight.

In my sestina, "Anniversary Poem," I generate the speaker's
bored playfulness and her wonderment over loving a man who
seems always to ignore her by playing with syntax. Her love is
compared to a nest:

> Her nest is not soft yet has such a smooth center
> love's fledglings sometimes slip and fall backwards
>
> flapping like a question asked backwards:
> "Him watch and here sit I do why?" He reads the paper.

Milton's sonnet, "On His Blindness," employs complex syntax
to ratchet up tension, putting more and more distance and
thought between the opening dependent clause, *When I
consider...*, and its logical almost-resolution eight lines later, *I
fondly ask.* For all its complexity, Milton's syntax is still,
amazingly, standard, while E. E. Cummings' unconventional
syntax often takes a reader right over the grammatical edge.
Cummings uses tricks with syntax to release energy that would
otherwise stay trapped in common usage. Like the splitting of
an atom, his language explodes:

> why must itself up every of a park
> anus stick some quote statue unquote to
> prove that a hero equals any jerk
> who was afraid to dare to answer no?

Such word-play eventually weaned me off *MAD Magazine* and
gave me Shakespeare—and I still love John Lennon, Edward
Lear, and Alfred E. Neuman.

Here are suggestions for sharpening your awareness of syntax:

1. Carl Phillips, whose training in classical languages influences his athletic syntax, joked during a reading about how he spends his weekends: at home, trying to write a poem of just one sentence. It's a safe weekend activity—one long sentence—and worth a try.

2. Write a poem of syntactical repetition, repeating the same arrangement of words, to create a special music, as in May Swenson's well-known poem "Question":

> Body my house
> my horse my hound
> what will I do
> when you are fallen
>
> where will I sleep
> how will I ride
> what will I hunt ...

Prompt and Poem

Ode to Gray

Mourning dove.
Goose. Cat bird. Butcher bird. Heron.
A child's plush stuffed rabbit. Buckets. Chains.

Silver. Slate. Steel. Thistle. Tin.
Old man. Old woman.
The new screen door.

A squadron of Mirage F-1's dog fighting
above ground-fog. Sprites. Smoke.
"Snapshot gray" circa 1952.

Foxes. Rats. Nails. Wolves. River stones. Whales.
Brains. Newspapers. The backs of dead hands.

The sky over the ocean just before the clouds
let down their rain.

Rain.

The sea just before the clouds
let down their nets of rain.

Angel fish. Hooks. Hummingbird nests. Battleships.
Teak wood. Seal whiskers. Silos. Railroad ties.

Mushrooms. Dray horses. Sage. Clay. Driftwood.
Crayfish in a stainless steel bowl.

The eyes of a certain girl.

Grain.

—Dorianne Laux

The use of color in a poem immediately creates visual imagery. A dull poem can be enlivened by some dashes of color. But gray? Such a dull color. Or so we might think. In this poem Laux rescues gray and makes it wonderful. How does she do this?

For one thing, the poet uses a long and varied list of things that are gray. Notice how strategically the items in the list are organized and how contrast is employed. Something delicate is followed by something harsh, e.g., the delicate *Hummingbird nests* is followed by the harsh *Battleships*. Also, a long item is followed by a short item. The list leads up to the enigmatic *eyes of a certain girl*, which moves the poem beyond mere list and leaves us wondering, What kind of love is this?

Laux also brings in the music of repetition and rhyme. The phrase *just before the clouds let down their rain* is repeated twice, with a slight addition the second time. The word *rain* is repeated three times and rhymes with *Chains, Brains, stainless,* and *Grain*. Notice all those *a* sounds there and in *dray, sage, clay,* and *crayfish*. There's also the music of alliteration, e.g., in *Butcher bird* and *Buckets* and in *Silver. Slate, Steel. Sprites. Smoke. / "Snapshot gray" circa.*

Finally, Laux discards sentences. Not one complete sentence in the poem. She also varies stanza length from three lines to one line of just one word. The fragments keep us moving. The stanza breaks make us pause.

Here's your challenge for your own monochromatic ode. First, select a color. You might want a dull color, e.g., brown, beige, tan, navy blue, white, maroon, or you might want a snazzy color.

Brainstorm a list of items in your color. Keep it going as long as you can. Think of animals, birds, jewels, pieces of clothing, food, flowers. Look around the room and find some more items to include. Don't quit until you've surprised yourself several times.

Freewrite about your feelings for this color. Any memories to include?

Now arrange your items in a sensible but seemingly random order. Capture the feelings in there without stating them. End with an emotionally resonant image.

Now go back and heighten the sound effects. Can you get in some rhymes, some near rhymes, some alliteration?

Do you feel that using a color is not allowing you enough latitude for originality? Change it up and try a sound, a taste, a texture. Go through the same process. Or go negative. Make your color or chosen subject thoroughly unappealing. Write an anti-ode.

Sample Poems

Ode to Yellow

Canary.
Gosling. Bumblebee stripe. The eyes of blackbirds.

Citrine. Pollen. Residue of saffron. The brick road in Oz.
Gold.

Dandelion & harvest moon. Butter & whipped honey.
The middle child traffic light. Chardonnay. Cowardice.
The cabin's porch light. A newborn's jaundice.

Eagle's feet. Iodine. Goldenrod in a mason jar.
Custard. Fireflies. Gingko trees in wintertime.

Sunflowers.
Their lover.

Egg yolks. Telephone books. Black-eyed Susans. Bruises.
Crime scene police tape.

Legal pads my father used to write upon.

German postal bikes. The Beatles' submarine.
Taxi. Hydrant. Urine. Toenail fungus.

Her fingertips after twenty years of inhaling.
Parchment just before burning.

Flames.

—Kelly Cressio-Moeller

Ode to Beige

Tumbleweed.
Desert sand. Dry grass. Owl.
O'Keeffe's New Mexico cliffs.

Calf. Coyote. Cocoon. Fawn.
A newborn's skin. A newborn's bones.
The latex gloves of delivery.

Coffee swirled with cream.
Lace. Lamp shades. Matchsticks.
Bare limbs on leather.

Tree bark. Biscuits. Rye bread.
Lips unpenciled and cracked.

Khakis swishing through clouds
of moonlit dust.

Dust.

Marble floor sprinkled with dust.

Mushrooms. Maplewood. Baseballs. Acorns.
Eye shadow. Pantyhose.
Almonds. Camels. Chinchillas.

Pampas grass in a ten gallon crock.

Crust.

—Constance Hanstedt

The Poet on the Poem: Ann Fisher-Wirth

It Was Snowing and It Was Going to Snow

Unseasonal weird once in a green moon Mississippi beauty—
deep deep snow. We woke early, dressed,
walked through the silent town and Bailey's Woods
to Faulkner's house, before anyone but a deer
had made prints, we trudged through abundance.
I held my husband's arm down the uneven trail,
the snow-mound stairs of the woods,
because I was afraid to fall, knowing how suddenly
bones break. Again and again when I touch him
I am filled with joy for the sheer fact of him
among all the infinite spaces—this burly,
beetle-browed man with the muscular legs
and fine-pored skin. Now, through my window,
grays and taupes of gingko and maple,
fractals of branches softened and warmed with snow,
then the greens of privets massed shabby beyond them,
and way down the hill, the Methodist Church
just barely red, a smudge through the trees. Someone
has built a snowman, someone is romping with a dog.
Soon night will climb the hill outside the window
where I wait for the white bees to swarm,
surrounding the branches, the house,
surrounding my sleep, scattering their cold pollen again.

DL: Tell us about your title's allusion to Wallace Stevens's "Thirteen Ways of Looking at a Blackbird." Why those lines for your poem? What do you think they add to your poem? At what point did they occur to you as just right for the title?

AFW: In Mississippi, we get heat that will fry your eyeballs and humidity that will curl your toes. The spring and fall are balmy, and it almost always freezes for a while each winter. Nearly every year, there's a smattering of snow that melts almost as soon as it falls. But we hardly ever have the chance to imitate a Northern climate, such as Wallace Stevens refers to in "Thirteen Ways of Looking at a Blackbird." We hardly ever have real snow, deep snow, strange and continuing snow. This is why the title stolen from Stevens seemed right, once it popped into my head. The overnight snow reached shin-high—and best of all, we could tell it would not immediately be over. It was snowing and then it stopped, yet we knew it was still going to snow.

DL: The syntax of your first line is immediately arresting and engaging. How did you arrive at that line? What kind of revision did it undergo? Or was it a gift?

AFW: This poem began as a prose freewriting; in the lull after Christmas, when I had a lot of free time before the new semester began, I vowed I would keep a journal every day. Since not much was happening except weather, I wrote about weather. I wanted to write a poem from this day's prose paragraph and to begin the poem with a rush and tumble of adjectives to convey how surprising, how wonderful this snow was. The line just leapt into my mind. I have to admit, the next day I nearly cut the line. Why? My hyper-rational mind took over and told me there is no such thing as a *green moon* or even a saying *once in a green moon*. Luckily, someone told me I was crazy.

DL: Your use of pronouns is intriguing and subtle. You begin with, in line 2, the first person plural *We*. In line 6, you split that pronoun in half and speak as *I*. This allows a shift from description of landscape to contemplation of love, that is, love for the other half of the *We*. What's said in these middle lines could only be said by the singular *I*. This movement from exterior to interior also parallels the action of the poem. Finally, this shift brings warmth into a poem about snow. Was any of this on your mind when you made the switch? What was your intention?

AFW: The *We* at the poem's beginning refers to my husband and me; we took a walk together. The *I* takes over when I begin to contemplate my feelings. You are right that the poem shifts at that point to become more inward; I did intend that, as I wanted the poem to expand beyond narrative or description to include this realm of self-awareness about feelings. I broke my knee about ten months before the day of this snowfall, and I'd had surgery and a long recovery. That made my progress down this specific snow-covered trail slow and careful, but it also made me intensely aware of the everyday gifts—starting with life itself. But that is the nature of *I* and *we* anyway. My thoughts are always solitary, even if what I am thinking about is the person walking beside me.

DL: What governed your line breaks? Also, I can see spots where your poem might have been broken into stanzas. Why did you opt for one stanza?

AFW: In this poem most of the line breaks are syntactic, yet there is quite a bit of enjambment; only three of twenty-three lines end at the end of a sentence. I wanted a fluid, meditative quality to infuse the narrative, which describes a single arc from daybreak to gathering night. This is why, though the poem is broken into sentences rather than being one long continuing sentence, there are no stanza breaks, and the sentences are handled with variously placed caesurae. One of my favorite poems in the world is Robert Frost's "After Apple-Picking," and it just occurs to me that his poem, too, enacts an arc in a single stanza (admittedly partly through flashback) from sleep to waking to impending sleep.

DL: The *white bees* metaphor that closes the poem is so wonderful. How did you land on that?

AFW: My children had a beautiful book, illustrated by Susan Jeffers, of Hans Christian Andersen's *The Snow Queen*. The Snow Queen comes to little Kai to carry him off in a blur and flurry of snow like bees. That, of course, is a malevolent image. But it lingered in my mind for its beauty and—if snow is likened to bees—in some weird way, its potential fertility and sweetness. Also, like the blank white screen with the film projector running that always used to come at the end of my father's slide shows, the snow-bees create an atmosphere of obliteration that is both ominous and comforting.

Bonus Prompt: Five Words on a Wire Poem

Make a quick but thoughtful list of five words, e.g., *broken, leaves, summer, fingers, startled.* Then give yourself 10-15 minutes to use all five words in a one-sentence poem.

Feel free to lift five words from a poem or piece of prose that's near at hand. Or just look at the table in front of you, or out the window, and grab the first five things you see.

Be sure to use just one sentence. You'll be surprised by the twists and turns this requirement leads to.

In your revision, you may abandon whatever isn't working and add whatever might work.

This is a terrific warm-up prompt and has the added benefit of often leading to a keeper poem.

VIII. Line / Stanza

Art is the only way to run away without leaving home.

—Twyla Tharp

Craft Tip #21: Ten Tips for Breaking Lines in Free Verse

—Wesley McNair

Where to break the line? Certainly, that is one of the most challenging issues we poets face, especially if we are writing free verse. In formal verse there are rules to guide us and rhymes to achieve. But in free verse the breaks must be guided by other principles. Most of us wrestle with this issue as we revise and revise.

Here are some suggestions for breaking lines:

1. Break your lines to suggest the mind at work shaping the poem, because every poem is a process of thought.

2. The poem is also about things that happen. Break to increase your reader's anticipation about what will happen next.

3. Break to suggest your poem's mood. For an openness of expression, try a long, end-stopped line. To create uncertainty or suspense, combine short lines with a long sentence, revealing and concealing as you go. For a mood of agitation or excitement, try a variable line length with a jagged margin.

4. Break to create a tension between the line and the sentence, remembering that the interplay of the two is the central drama of free verse, each having a different purpose. Consider the words of Charles Simic: *The line is Buddha; the sentence is Socrates.*

5. Think of your poem as a musical score, in the way Denise Levertov recommended, using lines to emphasize vocal rhythm and the pitch of intonation, and line breaks as short intervals of silence or rests.

6. Break so your reader sees how to say your poem.

7. But don't forget the wordlessness around the poem, which can be made articulate by a line break or by an artful arrangement of lines.

8. Break mainly on nouns, verbs, and the words that describe them; they carry the sentence's essential meaning.

9. In your line breaking imitate the stresses of meditation and feeling, which are present in every earnest and intimate conversation and are the true source of the line break.

10. Believe these tips and don't believe them. Let the feeling life of your poem be the final authority.

Poem and Prompt

Second Year of Marriage

Over breakfast and the staggering waft
of jasmine tea and pesto eggs, you say

if it were your job to create the senses,
you would have forgotten smell.

I keep my mouth shut, look
intrigued. A link to the limbic,

the olfactory: the pulse-quickening
scent-coffee, green-humid air, exhaust—

of the airport in Venezuela—or the way
the geranium in my living room sends me

straight back to my grandparents' deck,
those summer lunches. Last year,

I would have tried to convince you
of smell's virtues. Instead, I let it be.

Later, we fight over the best way to unlock
the car. No matter. Your scent, that wordless

telegram, still takes me apart, like it did
when it first arrived out of nowhere.

—Marie-Elizabeth Mali

What intrigues me in this poem is the poet's use of smell. We are very accustomed to visual imagery, but not so much to olfactory imagery. And yet smell is such an important sense. When I read the lines about the geranium taking the speaker right back to her grandparents' deck, I knew just what she meant, that is, how closely tied to past experience smell can be. There's a certain kind of wet morning that takes me back to Red Raider Camp with its vile man-made lake full of frogs and mud. The morning smell triggers my childhood memory, along with a sense of revulsion and a keen ache of nostalgia. Whenever I smell lilies of the valley, I remember my mother's Muguet des Bois, my mother all dolled up to go to Canasta Club.

Let's see how the sense of smell might work for you in a poem.

Write down the names of some sensuous food items, ones with fabulous aromas.

Write down some other items with strong, distinctive smells.

Let one or more of these items trigger a memory. Go back to another time and place. Freewrite about this.

Is there another person in your present scene and/or in the past scene? Write about this person.

Let this be a love poem, though it doesn't have to be a romantic love poem. Put yourself in the mood.

Now pull your material into a draft that shifts back and forth between past and present. Try just speedwriting at first. Give yourself ten minutes.

Shape your material into a poem, maybe eventually using 2-line stanzas as Mali has.

Sample Poems

The Scent of Orange Blossoms

My father braked hard,
kicked the car door open,
and dancing, disappeared
into the orchard
yelling, do you smell them,
do you smell—and into my
freeway-leaded childhood
the scent of orange blossoms
wafted like a stranger's
perfume.

—Erica Goss

Scents of Summer

We had summer vacations in a Greek
mountain village, my father's birthplace.

The old bus picked us up
at the train station,

rode past the sulfur
springs spa stench,

on to the foothills of the mountain,
where it climbed the tight switchbacks.

Scents of amaranth bush, sage, wild oregano,
and mountain tea filled the thinner air layers.

We'd stop at the goat-milk cookie
factory. Feta cheese and

freshly-dug onion scents from
farmers' bags filled our nostrils.

Higher up the mountain,
before the village line,

we'd get the first smell of the fir
forest and the flocks of sheep

resting in their folds, before we
arrived at our grandparents' home.

That was long ago, but I can still
remember, the signature duo of our arrival—

the horses' barn next door and
grandma's bread oven across the yard.

We entered the home in a fusion of smells—
air-dried sausage hanging from rafters,

chestnut wood logs burning
and glasses filled with resin wine on the table.

—Basil Rouskas

Craft Tip #22: Stanza Shuffle

—Sydney Lea

The tip I offer here may sound at once mechanical and eccentric, an odd combination to be sure. But it suggests a strategy I use not just sometimes but always, and it does work for me (when it works: I'd be lying if I told you every germ of a poem ended in triumph).

I will write a draft of whatever it is that comes out. I don't let myself stop. And I don't worry too much about lyrical language, figuration, line breaks, that sort of thing. I can deal with such matters later.

As a formalist poet—sort of—I seem able to write most unimpededly in some regular meter, but I don't worry about that either, nor do I necessarily recommend it if it doesn't fit your own inclinations.

When the pen—or in my case the computer keys—seems to have run its course, I sit back and count the lines I have laid down. Let's imagine they amount to fifty. Hmmm. What does the poem look like if I break it into five 10-line stanzas? If that process doesn't trip any notions, suggesting, say, how each stanza can be both self-contained and in organic relation with the whole, then what about ten 5-line stanzas? And ditto. Of course, I could do seven 7-line stanzas, either cutting a line or giving the fiftieth its own line in conclusion. You get the idea.

Then I may notice which of my meters appears to prevail. If I see a lot of hexameter, maybe I'll try to make the whole poem hexametric and see what that does.

Maybe, having chosen, let's say, the 10-line stanza format, I'll note that in one of those stanzas lines 3, 7, and 9 make rhymes or, more likely, half-rhymes. I try that on all the other stanzas, too. What gives after I do?

As I said, this does indeed sound mechanical, and in some sense it surely is. But it keeps me from worrying too early on about what the poem is about. The greatest danger, as I have noticed both in writing and in teaching, is for the poet to try too strenuously to *mean* something at a preliminary phase of composition. Much better to get lost in one's material, not in some *idea*, but rather in language itself.

In short, these strange little games of mine are just that: they are play. And I have found that by playing around with my material, I am often led in directions I had never imagined. If I want, using the imaginary model above, to rhyme the last word of line 3, which is *miracle*, with the last word of line 7, then I find that *lyrical* fits, and the very idea of lyricism becomes somehow a theme in the poem, as I wouldn't have foreseen.

You see, I have this weird but, in my experience, validated faith that if I surrender myself to my own words, the ones that came without too much cogitation or premeditation, they will lead me to a place I didn't know I'd be visiting; they will show me 1) What I didn't know was on my mind when I started, and 2) What I didn't know I knew about that particular subject.

The thrill of poetry, at least for me, lies in these unanticipated discoveries. And don't forget: you are allowed and encouraged to cheat on your own rules if to do so takes you to one of those unanticipated places. My little sandbox shufflings open me up to such discoveries, as the solemn effort at philosophical concept or intellectual conclusion simply can't do.

Poem and Prompt

Two Gates

I look through glass and see a young woman
of twenty, washing dishes, and the window
turns into a painting. She is myself thirty years ago.
She holds the same blue bowls and brass teapot
I still own. I see her outline against lamplight;
she knows only her side of the pane. The porch
where I stand is empty. Sunlight fades. I hear
water run in the sink as she lowers her head,
blind to the future. She does not imagine I exist.

I step forward for a better look and she dissolves
into lumber and paint. A gate I passed through
to the next life loses shape. Once more I stand
squared into the present, among maple trees
and scissor-tailed birds, in a garden, almost
a mother to that faint, distant woman.

—Denise Low

In this poem the speaker does what we so often do, that is, she
looks back at the person she once was. The poet imitates this
journey by having the speaker encounter her own reflection in a
glass window.

What might you look into that would reflect your image—pond,
store window, glass frame over a painting, TV screen,
someone's sunglasses, someone's eyes? Put yourself in front of
that reflector and bring forth the person you used to be.
Imagine a younger you. What might you be doing?

As you begin your draft, bring in some images from the earlier scene. Remember that you, as speaker, look with full knowledge. But the younger self does not see you or know of your existence.

After you've fully exploited the earlier scene, return to the present and bring in some images from that scene.

Notice the format that Low uses. The poem is 15 lines, sonnet-like with its two-part division. There is a logical break or turn that separates the two stanzas. See if you can achieve that.

Sample Poems

Behold

I look in the mirror, see the young
me in a sleeveless striped dress, brown
eyes shadowed by the newest product
along cosmetic aisles, sun-streaked hair
untouched by salon foils, tanned arms
with a curved silhouette that outlines
muscles toned with soup cans.

I download digital photos, see
an old woman, neck folds in strings
like melted mozzarella, cheekbones
that crave rediscovery, lines
in parentheses around lips
that forget to blush.

The young me speaks to the old me,
she speaks in fifties music that rolls
off her tongue as easily as the ABCs,
Sh Boom, walk down by the river,
a little white cloud cries for you.

The old me answers
  Yadadadadadadadadada,
  Sh Boom Sh Boom,
grandchildren in the other room
frightened by the songburst.
Ma, my daughter says, *your poodle*
skirt called, it wants you back.
I smile, think how life
could be a dream, a dream.

     —Gail Fishman Gerwin
      published in *Adanna Literary Journal*

Face to Face

From Grandmother's Waverly farm,
I've inherited the antique mirror.
I witness: a flat-chested girl
with my dimple, my curls.

She loathes her image, has cut
her arm, harbored more menacing
measures. In her dreams, she runs
from black wolves with bared teeth.

I tell her:
Before you do the dishes,
paint your nails cha cha coral.
Buy toucan green socks.

I tell her:
Go to the movies at noon.
Play Mozart quartets.
Be a good mother to yourself.

I tell her:
Your children will swirl
in dreams without wolves.

—Nancy Bailey Miller

The Poet on the Poem: Matthew Thorburn

Still Life

Pierre Bonnard

That he would go back
after hours to retouch
the ones hanging in the gallery—
he must have had an in
with the guards—to get it righter
if never right, you've heard
before. How he'd revisit
the light—bring it up
or turn it down—just as I have
returned to this morning
all afternoon. They make me
hungry, these two pears
he must have hurried to paint
so she could eat. A few green ideas
about grapes. The apple
shows off its high bald head.
To be fascinated by fruit.
Not fruit, but light. Imperfect mirrors,
imitation mirrors. His broken
pinks and reds, green and
yellow mottle, this dash of white—
no, light—no, canvas
showing through. I almost catch
my face there, looking back.
I know this fruit. I've eaten it
all my life, though this basket's
new to me—a few brown twists
of vine, uncertain transport
but I'm moved. I'll say that.
Made to speak. Such
tenderness, his abiding

affection for anything touched
by light. And he needed
so little. A few pieces of fruit.
A window. The sky
trying on every possible blue.

DL: Tell us something about the impetus behind this ekphrastic poem. What compelled you to attempt to enter the painting, to repaint it with words?

MT: A few years ago, I took part in a weekend poetry workshop in Manhattan where we were given an assignment to complete during our lunch break: go find a place to eat and write, then come back with a new poem to share with the group. Faced with this deadline, I ducked into a nearby Chinese restaurant and turned—in a panic—to my go-to poetry prompt: write about art.

I like poems that emphasize visual details and enable you to really see things—colors, shapes, light and shadow—so writing about paintings comes naturally to me. Sitting in that restaurant and staring at my blank page, I thought of Pierre Bonnard, one of my old favorites, and his light-filled interior scenes. I remembered, too, this sort of famous story about him: he had a habit of going back to his paintings to add a little more color, make something lighter or darker, or change some detail he wasn't happy with—even after they were hanging in galleries or shows. I remembered Jane Hirshfield has a poem that describes this painterly form of revising as *Bonnarding*. Since I was working from memory, my poem doesn't match up exactly with a specific painting of Bonnard's, but I tried to convey the feel of his work and some of my feelings about it. As I say in the poem, after looking at and thinking about his paintings, I was *made to speak*.

DL: I'm intrigued by the introduction of *she* in line 14. Why did you hold her back and then give her no further mention in the poem?

MT: There's that place where all the wonderful ambitions of trying to express yourself creatively run up against the practical business of everyday life, and that's a place that always interests me. Whatever musical phrase or clever line break I'm just about to get right as I revise a poem, dinner still needs to be cooked, the dishwasher emptied. I still have to go to work every day. Being aware of this friction is partly a way of staying grounded, and it makes the act of writing a poem that much more meaningful. I guess I was imagining the same was true for Bonnard, too: as a painter he may have seen these pieces of fruit as colors and shapes to be explored in paint, but to Marthe, his wife—she's the *she* I had in mind—they were apples and pears, there to be eaten. I hope a little note of thoughtful tenderness comes through, too, in the way he hurries his work along so she can have her lunch.

Marthe appears in many of Bonnard's paintings. These paintings aren't portraits exactly, but they wouldn't be the same without her. I suppose I thought she could nonchalantly and fleetingly appear in my poem, but in a way that felt important to me for the ballast she provides. For me, though, the poem is mostly concerned with what a strange thing it is to be so focused on one activity—in this case painting, being fascinated by light—and to feel that obsessive urge to get it right on the canvas.

DL: While you make only one brief reference to the *she*, you make ample use of repetition. *Light* and *fruit* both appear four times. Then you repeat sounds as in the rhyme of *right, white*, and *light*. The same sound is echoed in the assonance of *I, ideas, high, life, vine, abiding, sky, trying*. Tell us how you crafted these musical effects.

MT: I appreciate you noticing the music of the poem, because that's something I strive for as a writer and admire as a reader. I love rhymes and off-rhymes that fall within lines, as well as assonance, repetitions and echoes, and all the rhythmic effects you can produce with patterns of long and short lines, or by using phrases and fragments of sentences.

I usually write and revise out loud when I'm working at home, so I can hear how lines sound. Of course, I couldn't do that in the restaurant, but surely did later on when typing up the poem and revising it.

DL: As I read this poem, I feel as if I'm witnessing a mind at work, reaching and stretching for what it wants to say. I think your use of syntax is responsible for this effect. There's the reversed order in the first sentence which covers seven lines. That's followed by several fragments, several sentences broken by the use of dashes, and a few declarative statements followed by their negation, e.g., *To be fascinated by fruit. / Not fruit, but light.* Was all of this intuitive or crafted?

MT: I love the way certain poems convey the sense of a mind at work, the poet working out her or his thoughts—saying something, hesitating, backtracking and correcting—as the poem moves forward word by word. That's something Elizabeth Bishop probably invented in her "Poem," when she interrupts her own methodical, detail-by-detail description of a faraway landscape—it's a poem about a painting—to exclaim, *Heavens, I recognize the place, I know it!* So I was definitely conscious of striving for a similar effect in different ways throughout the poem.

But there's also the fact that I was on the spot there, with a short window in which to get my poem down on paper, so what shows through in the poem is also my effort to get to the heart of the thing.

DL: What made you choose the single stanza form?

MT: I wrote the first draft of this poem quickly—for me, anyway—and so it felt like one long thought or breath. As I work on a poem, I usually try different line breaks or stanza breaks until I find the form that feels right for that particular poem. Certain poems need some air and light to shine in between stanzas, to give the reader those pauses for breath or that little extra emphasis of a stanza break, as opposed to a line break. But here I wanted to hold the focus in this lingering moment, so it's one long breath and then it's done.

Bonus Prompt: The American Sentence Poem

The American Sentence was invented by Allen Ginsberg in response to the strict rules of the 3-line Japanese haiku with its 5-7-5 syllables pattern.

An American Sentence is a single sentence of seventeen syllables. For this prompt you will write a poem made up entirely of American sentences.

Example:

> Dead things litter the grass—branches,
> Leaves, needles—last summer's detritus.

To begin, imagine yourself looking out a window. Or actually do so.

Write your own American sentence using what you see outside that window.

Now write another that picks up from the first and so on.

At some point you might want to let a memory enter, to be transported to another time or location.

You will find that while this assignment is rule-heavy it will sharpen your perceptions and compel you to pay attention to syllables, sounds, and syntax. Because each sentence leads to the next, you should get some inner structure working.

Once you feel that you have a solid first draft, consider rearranging the order of the sentences. Now you can break the chains a bit if you like. Is there one sentence that has an unnecessary syllable? Get rid of it. Need a few more in another sentence? Add them. Try letting each sentence be a stanza, but consider how many lines you want per stanza.

IX. Revision

It's a funny thing, the more I practice the luckier I get.

—Arnold Palmer

Craft Tip #23: Opening the Too-Soon-Finished Poem

—Jeanne Marie Beaumont

A common issue that comes up a lot in student poems and my own work is closing the poem before it's really finished its work. We may get a great ending line and become over-eager about putting it into the poem, and then we rush. Or *something* makes us want to be escape artists of our poems rather than inhabitants and, because we are verbally smart and clever, we can always find a neat little key to let ourselves out of the poem and make it *sound* finished before the deeper issues are completely explored. False ending, over-closure, too neat a snap—you have probably done all of these at some time, as have I. It's like we've wrapped the gift box but forgotten to include the real present inside. A vague feeling of dissatisfaction may settle in.

Take your wedge and hatchet from your toolbox and hack open the poem. The best place to do that is usually before the final stanza, or if no stanzas, wherever the poem made its final turn into closing. Typically somewhere before its last quarter. Break the poem open, physically, there, and write into the empty space for a while. Write as much as you can.

To get you going, it may help to insert a word such as *But, Or, Meanwhile, Although, Yet,* or even *On the other hand.* Or write the negation of the last sentence before the *wedge space* and write off that. Whatever it takes to generate some furthering of your text. Write until you discover something you didn't know about the poem.

You may only wind up adding a line, or you might wind up with several, or you may take what you have written and knead it back into the poem, but if you apply yourself to this with the ardor of a self-prodder, always asking, *Is that all you have to say? Are you sure you've gotten everything into it? Anything else?* you will be able to take your poem, as I like to say, further, deeper, wilder.

207

Poem and Prompt

Fireflies

And these are my vices: impatience, bad temper, wine,
the more than occasional cigarette,
an almost unquenchable thirst to be kissed,
a hunger that isn't hunger
but something like fear, a staunching of dread
and a taste for bitter gossip
of those who've wronged me—for bitterness—
and flirting with strangers and saying sweetheart
to children whose names I don't even know
and driving too fast and not being Buddhist
enough to let insects live in my house
or those cute little toylike mice
whose soft grey bodies in sticky traps
I carry, lifeless, out to the trash
and that I sometimes prefer the company of a book
to a human being, and humming
and living inside my head
and how as a girl I trailed a slow-hipped aunt
at twilight across the lawn
and learned to catch fireflies in my hands,
to smear their sticky, still-pulsing flickering
onto my fingers and earlobes like jewels.

—Cecilia Woloch

The first thing that strikes me about this poem is its long list.
Let's try a list poem, also called a *catalog poem*.

For the first draft begin as Woloch does with the words, *And
these are my* _____ :

In the blank space substitute the topic of your list poem, e.g., virtues, wishes, sins, secrets, transgressions, dreams. Before you begin your draft, brainstorm a long list of examples that illustrate your topic. Work quickly. Let the list be varied.

Begin drafting the poem. You might want to just begin at the beginning of your list, or you might want to first think about order. Save the best item for last (but make them all good, of course). Notice the contrast in Woloch's last vice. Such a lovely image of destruction. End your own poem with a strong image, not with information.

Notice the syntax. Woloch's poem is one long stanza and one long sentence. That adds intensity. Consider using the same strategy as well as the varied line lengths. Or you might want to go in just the opposite direction and use stanzas and multiple sentences that are fairly even in length.

For an alternative approach, try this beginning: *And these are your_____:*

Sample Poems

And this is my loneliness:

coming home to cold rooms,
our unmade bed, piles of dirty clothes,
unopened bills, casseroles rotting with grief.

Nothing tastes. I eat crackers for dinner, and worry
about our girls who will stumble and grow old without
your patience, who will turn bitter with loss, and the baby
who will know only photos I show, each time saying
this is the man who tried to live longer just for you.

It's still raining. We're cold. The grass, even in winter,
is long and green, mocking our want. Every gray day,
every clear sky, every turn, everything
is reminder and wound.

There's no room in this emptiness.
Our bed is vacant. I sleep on the floor, dreamless
with the memory of late nights cocooned in you.

—Drew Myron
published in *Sweet Grief*

And These Are the Promises:

to almost burn listening to music, to glean
the swallow turning as one with his flock,

to wake to cathedral sounds
of ocean baptizing, burying the land,

to gather the peace sifting through firs in the yard,
my tongue of honey

or sometimes stone,
to breathe autumn's nip of apples;

above all else—forgiveness:
for yellow lights turning red, for wanting

to paint the hall but not knowing
ivory or ecru, for afternoons writing in my study

which isn't even mine but is, for living more
inside than out, for misplacing evermore

those childhood evenings when my sister and I
lay on the lawn and stared at the stars,

willing them to fall into our hands still aglow.

—Wendy Elizabeth Ingersoll

211

Craft Tip #24: In the Middle of Things

—Julie Kane

Poets of previous eras did not have to compete, as we do, with a host of different media ready to seduce away the attention of a bored reader. Yet they knew how to hook a reader's attention by beginning *in medias res*, that is, *in the middle of things.*

Sir Thomas Wyatt the Elder (1503-1542) begins a poem, *They flee from me*. Rather than waste a couple stanzas explicating who *they* are and why they are fleeing, Wyatt sweeps up his reader in a surge of adrenalin. The backstory will be revealed as the poem unfolds. Likewise, John Donne (1572-1631) grabs his reader by the throat with opening lines such as this: *For God's sake hold your tongue, and let me love.*

When we sit down to write a poem, we have to sweep away the trivial, ego-driven thoughts that preoccupy us throughout much of our waking lives. We have to drill down through bedrock in order to reach that vein of copper or silver or gold that is life at its most intense, experience charged with meaning. But while a miner would never dream of shipping thousands of tons of trash rock to a dealer in precious metals, too often we poets stay attached to the false starts of our poems, to the stanzas that only served to lead us from the banality of everyday life to the gleaming ore beneath the surface.

Revisit some of your poems. Where do they really begin—in the first stanza, or later on? Try revising one of them so that it begins *in medias res*, and see if you like the difference. After all, this literary technique was familiar to the ancient Greeks and Romans. Isn't it time you tried it?

Poem and Prompt

Rondeau After a Transatlantic Telephone Call

Love, it was good to talk to you tonight.
You lather me like summer though. I light
up, sip smoke. Insistent through walls comes
the downstairs neighbor's double-bass. It thrums
like toothache. I will shower away the sweat,

smoke, summer, sound. Slick, soapy, dripping wet,
I scrub the sharp edge off my appetite.
I want: crisp toast, cold wine prickling my gums,
love. It was good

imagining around your voice, you, late-
awake there. (It isn't midnight yet
here.) This last glass washes down the crumbs.
I wish that I could lie down in your arms
and, turned toward sleep there (later), say, "Goodnight,
love, It was good."

—Marilyn Hacker

Let's take on the challenge of a form poem, the rondeau. The form consists of a quintet, a quatrain, and a sestet. It has only two rhymes and one refrain. The rhyme scheme is aabba aabR aabbaR. In this pattern the *R* stands for *refrain*. The refrain consists of words taken from the beginning of the first line. Lines may be of any length and they may vary in length.

You can see in Hacker's rondeau that the first line is very important, so don't rush to get your first line. Notice how

Hacker's use of the word *love* changes somewhat with each subsequent appearance. As you compose your first line, consider words that have multiple meanings or that function as more than one part of speech.

Don't go for easy rhymes and feel free, as Hacker has, to use slant rhymes. Notice how Hacker uses line breaks and enjambment not only to achieve the rhyme scheme but also to achieve interesting shifts of meaning.

It is a common practice when working in an unusual form to incorporate the name of the form into the title. You might want to do that.

You may very well find that this poem forces you to stretch. While the rhyme scheme seems easy, to make it work effectively and with pleasing music will require some patience and revision.

Sample Poems

Return Rondeau

We walk through your city, this place where
years ago you breathed electric air,
talked God all night with friends and called it heaven.
Now streets are lined with Starbucks and 7-Elevens.
We walk through your city.

You look around for places that aren't there—
the old bookstore, the Golden Chair
Saloon, the grocery, the Lucky Seven—
as we walk through your city

which seems like nothing much, surely nowhere
one would remember. An old pair
of lovers quarrel, break apart. Not even
a bird sings in the autumn cold. Wind-driven
walkers hasten home. The trees are bare.
We walk through your city.

—Janet McCann

Rondeau Before Grading a Stack of Papers

Neatly typed and ready for review, a dreary
stack of essays waits near me,
begging to be graded—the final
efforts of my students to pull
excellence from their

individual wells of inspiration. Here,
now, I, too, am an ungraded paper,
a work-in-progress, crisp words all
neatly typed and ready for review.

What red marks, what notes for
revision will my margins harbor
to marshal my thoughts as I struggle
to produce my *magnum opus*—a feeble
draft, or words that will last forever,
neatly typed and ready for review?

—Thomas Moudry

Craft Tip #25: Revising: The Spider Web, the Fishing Net, the Hammock

—Lee Upton

Sometimes poems fail because the poet is being diligent in all the wrong places; the poet patches over any open spaces that might have allowed the unfamiliar to enter. The poem that results is static, a small, obedient poem, sadly *complete* in a limited sense. The poem is a clumsy solid.

When revising a poem, I find that three images are useful: the spider web, the fishing net, and the hammock. What all three physical forms have in common: strands connect around empty spaces. The silk or cord or rope resolves into a pattern that makes it possible for us to see the form and, at the same time, to see through the form. For a web or a net or a hammock to take shape, multiple strands must connect. For a poem to be dynamic, multiple levels of meaning must intersect. To make the most meaning within a poem, we probably should leave room for the unanticipated, for gaps in the weave of the poem.

The Spider Web

First, when revising, consider the spider web. A spider web isn't active. It doesn't have to be: it's sticky. A spider web may seem invisible until we walk into one. So, too, can the actual nature of a draft be invisible to us. We may think we know the draft but often we don't experience fully enough—and compassionately enough—what is on the page or the screen. And so before changing the poem, it might be best to let our attention become sticky. After all, why change the poem until you know the poem?

Read and reread to see what the draft is doing. No need to be aggressive yet. Follow the poem's contours. Even obvious errors may be valuable. Where is the poem *sticky* in the worst sense? That is, where do the dead flies among your words cling to the

217

poem? Where is the poem *sticky* in the best sense? That is, where does the imagination get caught and redeemed?

But, again, before changing the draft, wait. Be patient. Take the time to know your draft. Such attentiveness requires discipline. Respect the strange silky thing. One breath will change its shape.

See what you have before you sweep it away.

The Fishing Net

After using the image of the web, the image of the fishing net is in order. A fishing net presumes activity. A net can be tossed, fanning out upon the waters. A net can scoop. A fishing net can be lowered and then hauled to draw up what's far beneath the surface. (For this second revision step, be sure to keep each draft you create so that you can be astonishingly aggressive. When earlier versions are available, you won't need to fear losing anything.)

A first possibility: Haul up the last stanza of the draft and make it the beginning of a new draft. Start from the point that seemed to be the end, where you thought possibilities had been exhausted. Another experiment: Knot parts of the poem by adding more consonant sounds or make the poem muscular by experimenting with graphic verbs. Or let the poem, like a net, be sinuous; extend the poem. You could braid the poem by intertwining an additional subject or line of questioning. See what happens when subjects overlap and struggle within the poem. Or talk back to the poem on every other line. Continue to experiment with networks of connections. Could the poem be part of a series?

Another possibility: Shrink the poem. Or fold multiple drafts into one poem.

Or let the actual experience you're undergoing as you revise wriggle through the poem. That is, toss your net beyond the poem. Apply the image of the fishing net to your environment as you revise the draft. What outside the poem wants to enter the lines? What have you overheard while you were revising? Can something of the moment that you're experiencing become tangled in the next draft?

The Hammock

Finally, consider the hammock. A hammock is another form of net or web, secured above ground between two points. A hammock is designed for holding a body in comfort. And if you don't know how to get in or out of one, you may find yourself flailing.

Getting out of a poem—that's where poems are often marred, sometimes by impatience, or by grasping after profundity, or by a tendency to cap the poem with a pre-determined meaning. We get tired of waiting for an ultimate surprise and are tempted to settle for a substitution. We may get out of the poem but the poem hasn't gotten much out of us.

Getting out of a poem is far harder than getting out of a hammock, although there are some similarities in the process. Concentrate or you'll flip. Focus on positioning your body. Ask: Where is the body in this poem? What senses are active? What metaphors call up bodily images? And where are the poles of energy that keep the poem swaying? How is the poem meticulously balanced or provocatively unbalanced? Test the poem aloud repeatedly.

Then, finally, sleep on it.

If the poem hasn't surprised and gratified you already, you can start revising again at the next opportunity. First, try the sticky patience of a web, then the hard pull of the fishing net to draw the poem's mysteries to the surface. Then try the hammock and see how long you can stay in the poem, and if it will allow you—at last—to rest.

Poem and Prompt

Snake Lady

She was the main event when
    the carnival came to town.
Fourteen and oh, so young,
    we stood inside her tent with
boys who spoke among themselves
    of things that made them men.

Had we been older, we might
    have understood—their helpless
fascination as the snake slid
    between her breasts and made its
thick descent along her thighs.
    Those boys never blinked until
her fingers stroked the coils

straight, tightened on the head,
    and coaxed it to a sudden milky
venom. With an innocence we
    didn't think we had, we blushed
and turned from the sure and
    easy way she made them burn.

—Adele Kenny

Kenny's poem initially appears simple enough. The speaker describes a memory of something she observed when she was fourteen. However, the poet has built in several layers of complication. The speaker does not merely observe the scene; she observes someone else observing it. Then instead of using first person singular, the poet uses first person plural; a group of girls observes a group of boys observing an action. The poet also recounts the incident from the distance of Time. The speaker is no longer on the threshold of adolescence but is an adult looking back on the scene. As such, she can have perceptions that the fourteen-year-old girl could not have had. Finally, the entire poem rests on a metaphor, a very sexy one, indeed!

Let's see if we can do something similar. Let's begin with a simple draft and then add layers of complication.

First, choose a potentially sensuous and sensual scene to describe, perhaps someone eating a peach or a tomato, someone shampooing or bathing, someone turning on a water faucet or drinking from a fountain, someone planting bulbs or dancing or making a salad.

For your first draft, describe the scene, first person singular, present tense. The speaker can be you or someone you pretend to be. The action can be real or imagined.

Now let's add some layers to that basic draft. Complete each step before moving on to the next one.

1. Bring in a third character, someone to stand between the speaker and the person doing the action. Rewrite the draft so that your speaker not only describes the action but also observes and describes the new character observing the scene. Stick with first person singular and present tense.

2. Revise using past tense. The scene now becomes a memory.

3. Revise again, this time using first person plural. Who else could be with your speaker? Who else could be with the other observer?

Think about how each revision changes the poem. (For example, the shift in time, from present to past tense, might alter the tone of the poem.) Choose the version you like best and continue to work on that one. But keep all the steps in your arsenal.

Notice how Kenny indents every other line. That nicely parallels the back and forth between past and present and between the speaker and the other characters. Aim for a form that enhances meaning.

Sample Poems

Breakfast in Patmos, Greece

With serrated knife he peels the peach,
      its skin falling

onto the porcelain plate,
      the pulp wetting his palms. Every

morning begins this way. He
      has trained his fingers

to handle both tough and delicate fruits.
      An orange, a kiwi.

Carefully he carves
      the outer layers,

watches them tumble
      over each other,

the half-moon of an orange rind
      shading the speckled hull of a kiwi.

Eating is not
      the purpose,

but the artful exposure of flesh
      beneath.

          —Laura Freedgood
          published in *The Stillwater Review*

After the Funeral

She pulls open the drawer with both hands,
lifting up on the knobs to ease the wood's passage.

Her mother raises her head at the sound,
sees her daughter kneeling on the carpet

in front of the dresser he bought her years ago.
Inside, linens lie folded, cool, stacked

by function—fitted, flat, pillow covers.
From her chair, the mother sees the piles,

sees her daughter pause as a trace of potpourri
rises from the drawer into the air,

watches her reach in, slide her hands
under the sheets she's chosen, and lift them out.

She moves to help, but the daughter shakes her head.
She will make the bed herself. She stretches

each layer taut, smoothes it with firm fingers
pressed against the mattress.

Her mother watches her daughter's hands
fold hospital corners, precise and elegant.

They could have been her own hands.
Her daughter circles the foot of the bed,

back and forth, in an arc
like a hummingbird courting.

—Lisken Van Pelt Dus

The Poet on the Poem: Deborah Bogen

The Rudest Gesture is the Phone That Rings in the Night

Grant to my brother
that he come here unharmed.
Grant safe passage, that he arrive whole

and please grant to my brother,
        lost now among winds,
        among strange and unknowable winds

a refreshment of breath
that we know the hour of our true meeting,
        the hour of our last parting.

Grant him a moment's ease when the song spinning
in his skull is released,
when his throat softens and opens,

and although I am neither the honey nor the bee,
I ask that you grant me this:
        a dispelling of smoke for my brother
who has been homeward bound
for years.

Grant that he come, penniless or resurrected.
Raise before my face his scarred
and ink-stained palm.

Gently open his mouth once more,
one last time gently open him
that river music
flow.

DL: Your poem strikes me as a prayer for a brother's return and resurrection. Tell us about the nature of the resurrection and your use of implied biblical allusions.

DEB: I had a stepbrother who I met for the first time when I was fifteen and he was eleven. Despite our ages we were almost immediately bonded as siblings—we were that kind of personality match, I guess. We were close and we always knew the hour of our first meeting.

When I was writing this poem, he was dying of complications of Hepatitis C. He had been on the liver transplant list for some time, and I found out later was denied a new liver because he had continued to drink. I was sad, but I understood the transplant committee's decision. Anyone who keeps drinking with a failing liver does not really want the transplant. My brother didn't. That was a hard pill to swallow. I wanted him to stay with me on this planet, to be *resurrected* with a new liver, but he had been sick a long time. He wanted to let go.

The biblical allusion falls out of the Christian claim of Jesus' resurrection, of course, but the idea of coming back, of some sort of rebirth precedes Christianity. I was raised in a Christian Church and loved the exposure to the King James version of the Bible. A lot of that language is gorgeous—spell-binding you might say. When I found myself falling out of the religious life, when I was unable to take a great deal of it seriously, I still loved the language and I simply refuse to give it up.

DL: Your title seemingly has no connection to the poem, yet I feel it powerfully. Was there ever a point in your drafting when a phone was in the poem, when its ringing disturbed the night?

DEB: Every Monday night I write with a group of poets and fiction writers in a workshop in my living room. We all write together to a prompt and then read that work out loud. I run the group and sit by the phone. It is my job to remember to turn it off. But the phone itself is right there and in my mind as a potential disturbance. One night the prompt included something about *gesture*—to use gesture in the writing, perhaps to define or develop a character. I can't quite remember. In any case I found myself writing, *The rudest gesture is the phone that rings in the night*. The possible implications are obvious, but I found that the phrase itself kept coming back to me. It took months to realize it was related to my fears for my brother, to my desire to not get the call I knew had to be coming.

DL: I'm interested in your use of anaphora to structure the poem. *Grant* begins four lines and is embedded in two additional lines. The repetition adds rhythm and a tone that is both demanding and begging. Talk a bit about the craft decision that went into the use of this deceptively simple device.

DEB: It might be fair to say there was a decision to let that language stay in, and even overtake, the poem, but it came on its own in the first draft when I was writing freehand with a pen in a notebook. You are quite right to call out the demand and the begging which I think are part of our most desperate hours, when we are half imploring and half stamping our feet as if some kind of tantrum might turn the tide. I was worried about it sounding too Christian, too prayerful, but I used the repetition to invoke the casting of a spell. Can I cast that spell? Can I hypnotize the universe into supporting my project? Probably not but that impulse has fueled magic and religion for a long time. It is deeply human to wish to do it, I think.

I also used it to allow a heart-heavy outpouring, a saying and re-saying. It was meant to allow a river of feeling to flow without apology or justification. When we have to let go of a loved one, all our usual attempts to appear rational and grownup, even artful, seem ineffectual. We are the child again wanting it please, please, please.

DL: The poem has beautiful and intriguing images. Tell us about *his scarred / and ink-stained palms* and the final stanza's *that river music flow*.

DEB: I was surprised to find myself using *palms* but at some level I wanted to invoke a resurrection again, that late in the game when I should have been able to just let him go. Jesus' palms were scarred by his crucifixion in all the images from my childhood. I also wanted the palm raised up before my face, as in a goodbye gesture, a gesture that might soften the jangling of the phone with the bad news and give us one last moment of communication and understanding. One thing my brother and I both did was write songs so the ink was right there. He was a guitar player and somehow I always found those chords, his music, a wonderful wave, a flow of sound. Riverlike.

DL: The poem invites an oral reading, but I hear its music in my head. How much attention did you pay to the music? How did you achieve it?

DEB: You notice all the things a poet hopes will work. The music in the poem hopes to claim the music in prayers, in rituals, in spells. As I worked on it, I spent a lot of time saying it aloud, and revising. That kind of sound rehearsal is something you cannot do enough of, and I am always sorry when I read something in public that seemed quite good on paper and hear something that lets me know I sent it out before I had done all the work. It hurt to read this out loud, over and over, of course. I kept finding myself reaching for the Kleenex box and trying to stifle the tears as I worked. When I could read it while I was alone without being overtaken by emotion, I read it to my husband, and found myself struggling again. When the words move through the body, we find things out.

You didn't ask this, but I want to say that not too long before my brother died we got to spend a day singing, playing guitar, being our best selves together. He was tired and I knew I should go, but we played on because we both knew we were singing together for the last time. We were privileged to know the hour of our last parting and to say the goodbye my poem seeks. It doesn't fix everything or avoid pain, but it is a worthwhile thing to do. I hope that someday in our society we will be able to look death more squarely in the face so we can have our goodbyes in a setting that honors the lives we seek to lead and the loved ones we are lucky to have known. It's a hard thing to do. But then, most good things are.

Bonus Prompt: The Exploitation of a Metaphor Poem

Poets are weird. They don't see things as other people do. They don't see things as they really are. Instead, they are always thinking about what things are *like*. This exercise asks you to put on strange-colored glasses and practice metaphorical thinking as you draft a new poem.

Make a list of abstract words, for example, *jealousy, fear, sorrow*. Include words with emotional resonance. Avoid the very broad, idealistic abstracts such as *patriotism, justice, honor*. Let the words form a column.

Now, next to the first list, make a list of concrete objects, for example, *mirror, rock, artichoke*. Make the items specific.

Choose one abstract word from the first column and pair it with one concrete word from the second column. Turn the words into a metaphor, e.g., *Jealousy is an artichoke*.

Quickly create a bank of words you could use to describe the concrete object, e.g., *dark green, an armadillo of a vegetable, heart at the center, prickly leaves, so little meat, succulent, dipped in butter, stuffed with breadcrumbs*, and so on.

Use the metaphor as the first line in your poem. As you draft the poem, draw words and phrases from the word bank.

X. Writer's Block / Recycling

Writers don't retire. Writers never stop writing.

—Andy Rooney

Craft Tip #26: When the Poem Won't Show Up

—Ann Fisher-Wirth

I am prone to pretty severe writer's block, and I've often found that if I try to write something that looks like a poem right away, nothing happens. So I have become a believer in timed non-stop freewrites. This also works very well in a group; the results are often fantastic.

Here is how it goes: you choose, or your designated leader chooses, a short phrase. My favorite, and one that has led to several of my poems, is *In that kitchen*. But the phrase can be anything—even a single word like *blue*—though not an abstraction. You write it down and keep writing, without stopping, for 15-20 minutes. No editing, no crossing out, no judging. Whenever you get stuck, you go back to your starter phrase and continue to write it until other words emerge.

When the time is up, you end. Then you can either let the piece sit for a while or read it over to yourself or aloud. You may find that you have written a nearly finished prose poem. Or you may find that you have generated phrases, sentences, lines, images, that you can cull to use in a lineated poem. Or you may just tuck it away and discover sometime in the future that, lo and behold, something leaps out at you.

One lovely thing about fresh and interesting language is that it doesn't age. Language you generate now may find its place in a poem twenty years from now. And, of course, it may not—but there's always the next one.

Additional starter phrases:

I am standing at
I am thinking about
I remember
I didn't mean

Poem and Prompt

Missing You

The blue cheese dressing rattles
inside the refrigerator door, half-empty.
I thought about opening it,
drenching each red-green leaf,
just to fill my mouth
with something that you loved.

     —Jennifer Gresham

A lot gets accomplished here in just six lines. The title seems ordinary enough, but once we've read the poem we realize that it does a lot of work for the poem. It first sets up an expectation—this will be a poem about one person missing another, possibly a love poem, a sad one. But then we arrive at the first line and get a nice jolt—blue cheese dressing? Such a delightfully surprising image. How can it possibly relate to the title? Oh, but it does. Gresham works her image so skillfully that by the end of the poem we are aching with longing for the missing lover. Blue cheese dressing, indeed.

In an essay about *Hamlet*, T. S. Eliot speaks of the *objective correlative*. In his poem, *Paterson*, W. C. Williams includes his famous line: *No ideas but in things*. Both poets seem to be speaking of the use of a concrete object or objects to express a particular emotion. The object is associated with the emotion and is used to evoke that emotion in the reader. The emotion is objectified. You know that plaid shirt that always makes you think of your father? The early morning smell of wet grass that transports you back to summer camp? How about that doorknob and the day your lover left for good?

Let's see if you can pack this much power into six lines or thereabouts. Begin with a title that will express the situation or mood of your poem, e.g., *Wanting You, Hating You, Loving You, Forgetting You, After You Left.*

Then begin with an image that's mundane and seemingly unrelated to the topic suggested by your title. This should be something concrete. Place that image or object somewhere, e.g., on a shelf, in a closet, under the sink. Freewrite about the image. Explore it. Meditate on it. Colors, size, shape. Figure out a way to loop back to the title.

From this mass of writing, mine out a short poem. Try working with short lines. Perhaps just two sentences total.

Feeling contrary? Okay, then be expansive. Let this be a long poem with your image fully exploited, or perhaps a series of images to develop the idea of the title.

Sample Poems

Baggage

The black pocketbook you carried
the last few years of your life
sits in a corner of my closet
still holding those things
most dear to you—your fountain pen,
your tortoiseshell comb,
your embroidered handkerchief.
Maybe this is the year
I'll discard the purse,
lift every last item from it
until the worn leather hulk
collapses in my grip.

—Antoinette Libro

Worst

In a back-and-forth wind,
the showers hit different places
on the walls and skylights,
make different plinks and raps,
like an instrument of wood
struck by wood.

Caroling, the finches descant.

You go away. I come close
to the perilous edge. Down there
the rocks are far and hard,
the waves a million drummers
marching in all directions.

The finches trill their *whirst,*
whirst, whirst! They detonate decibels,
tiny firecrackers in the watery air.
Worst is their trill today.

You come back. The silence grows
small shoots on the walls
of the well my heart became.
Rain falls deeply in, musical.

I step back miles
from the cliffs, listening
to singular notes,
suddenly tall enough
to send out my own
from where I had tucked them
back inside.

—Rachel Dacus
published in *Kinship of Rivers*

235

Craft Tip #27: Saving the Savory

—Ingrid Wendt

Letting go is not, and never has been, something I do easily. Downsizing, three years ago, from a 1900 square foot house to just over 1000 square feet, nearly did me in. When it comes to poetry, though, I've somehow managed to accept—most of the time—the fact that crafting a diamond out of the rough draft of a poem often means leaving out certain gorgeous lines, or wonderful words, or stunning metaphors, or brilliant images that overburden the poem. Cut. Cut. Cut. Isn't that what we always hear from writing instructors, ourselves (sometimes) included?

But need these words be wasted? Thrown out, never to be seen again? Good news, all you who hate to toss: you can *repurpose* at least some of these words. And, oh happiness, some day you might use them again; they might even get you out of a jam.

Here's my system. Outmoded though it may be in today's digital age, the old-fashioned loose-leaf binder still serves as a place to keep those gems of words, lines, images, and ideas I've reluctantly tossed out. Prominent among the spines of books shelved next to the thesaurus, rhyming dictionary, and other reference books I keep above my desk, this special binder's front pages (ahead of entire first drafts of poems to return to some day) bear these headings: *Lines Saved, Lines for Future Poems, Favorite Words, Good Rhymes*, and *Images I Like*.

What good can this do? Here are two examples:

1. More than halfway through a rough draft of "On the Nature of Touch," which appears in my book, *Evensong*, I got stuck. Drew a total blank. I went to the notebook, leafed through it for a bit, and found an image—hair dye stains on the downstairs hall carpet like stones Hansel tossed to find the way home—which had come to me during a workshop on

236

metaphor I'd taught several years before. Whoopie! That worked! I was off and writing again.

2. Another poem from *Evensong*, "Silence," is a Cento: technically, a poem made entirely of lines cut from other poems. In my case, "Silence" is made of lines from several different notebook pages, not even close to each other, which I didn't realize resonated with each other and belonged together until I looked at them again in a moment of feeling totally dry and unable to complete the assignment I'd just given students at a retreat. Was this cheating? I did feel a bit guilty, at first. But the words were mine and putting them together anew made a poem I could be happy with.

These lists don't, of course, consist entirely of lines cut out of other poems. Sometimes I'll be doing the dishes or talking or listening to music, and I'll hear myself thinking a line that needs to be in a poem. Sometimes I think a poet is someone who doesn't think such terribly different thoughts from everyone else; it's just that we poets catch ourselves thinking them, and we recognize their potential. So if and when I can find some paper, I write them down.

Poem and Prompt

Compulsively Allergic to the Truth

I'm sorry I was late.
I was pulled over by a cop
for driving blindfolded
with a raspberry-scented candle
flickering in my mouth.
I'm sorry I was late.
I was on my way
when I felt a plot
thickening in my arm.
I have a fear of heights.
Luckily the Earth
is on the second floor
of the universe.
I am not the egg man.
I am the owl
who just witnessed
another tree fall over
in the forest of your life.
I am your father
shaking his head
at the thought of you.
I am his words dissolving
in your mind like footprints
in a rainstorm.
I am a long-legged martini.
I am feeding olives
to the bull inside you.
I am decorating
your labyrinth,
tacking up snapshots
of all the people
who've gotten lost
in your corridors.

—Jeffrey McDaniel

McDaniel's poem follows the tradition of the apology poem. The first line tells us what the speaker is apologizing for—his lateness. That simple statement is followed by a series of excuses, extravagant and unbelievable. Midway through the poem, the speaker switches from excuses to metaphors. We are left never knowing why the speaker was late or even what he was late for. Does some kind of truth perhaps reside in the lines about the father?

Notice how essential the title is to our understanding of the poem. It prepares us for the lies told in the poem and influences our response to them.

Notice that the speaker never reveals to whom he is speaking. It's possible, even likely, that McDaniel had a specific auditor in mind when he wrote the poem, but we don't know that.

Let's follow in McDaniel's footsteps and write an apology poem. First, pick something to be sorry about, e.g., forgetting someone's birthday, not showing up for a date, neglecting to feed the cat. You can be vague or specific about your error. You will increase the likelihood of capturing a strong voice if you have an auditor in mind, real or invented, even if you do not address or identify the auditor.

Brainstorm a list of excuses. Call forth your powers of invention. Let it get weird.

Now begin your poem with a simple statement of regret—*I am sorry for*, or *I regret*, or *Forgive me for*, or *I apologize*. Pick up from that opening line.

After two to three excuses, bring in a negative statement. Begin it with *I am not*. Then keep on going.

Then swing into metaphors of self-identification. Somewhere along the way, insert some kind of truth.

You might want to imitate McDaniel's skinny format. Or you might opt for longer lines and multiple stanzas. See what happens if you switch to third person.

Bonus points for bringing in an allusion or a cocktail.

Sample Poems

Mendacity (or Lies, Lies and More Lies)

I'm sorry I did not feed your cat.
I was skimming the waves
on the back of a dolphin.
I was hitching a ride
on an East River ferry
its fog horn keening through the dark.

I'm sorry I did not feed your cat.
The truth is I'm allergic to cats.
I concede he is splendid
in his Maine coon coat
but when he tiptoes across
the back of my chair
he creeps me out. When he cuddles my feet
and stares at me
I fear he's planning my demise.

I am not Brunhilde.
Ich bin ein Berliner.
I am an icy White Russian.
I am the Great Horned Owl
you saw in the forest
pumping its wild wings
when your father took you owling.

Under a frosty moon your feet crunched
over crisp snow and the two of you
hooted and hooted and hooted
until I hooted back. Your toes turned to stone
in your black boots. That was your old man
Grin and bear it ...
Mine? I am the owl who cursed his name.

—Liz Dolan

About Today

I'm sorry. I meant to call you back.
Who doesn't want to see a chick flick?

Heck, I'm a woman.
You're a woman.
We love mushy and sentimental.

Picture this:
Strong man grabs longing woman.
Zoom in on his chiseled face.
Then, pause.
Long, drawn out, 360 degree kiss.

Perhaps, if the movie were racy enough—
a lovely flash of the actor's bum.

Trust me, I'd much rather be with you
than sipping coffee at Panera Bread.

In fact, I planned to call you back,
but couldn't find anything to wear.

Attire is important, you know?

Certainly no jeans for the cinematic moment
when the lovebirds fade into the backdrop.

Yet a dress? Too much for the ride home
to my cat, queen-sized bed, the coziness
of sleeping without someone in my arms.

You see, I would have called you back,
but nothing, nothing, seemed to fit right.

—Kristina England

The Poet on the Poem: Nancy White

beauty

his copper hair his forearm glossy softening
waist scrotum rough his suddenly
attentive kiss his

monstrous appetite for meat his
whims analyzed and deified his hilarity
with children his tin voice his pursed

lips his backbeat rhythm his sigh when
he comes when he takes the first bite
his legs in black his tough rust

colored nipples his neck smelling of
narcissus his lack of hangnails his laugh like
a landmine such intention

of goodness his appearance golden his
tantrums his silence frozen after fine sex
cordial after bad his beauty his

beauty his darkness is love

DL: Why did you decide to omit punctuation and capitalization
in this poem?

NW: The issue of punctuation and capitalization was huge for
me in my book, *Detour*. The first poem, "Woven and Sewn," is
packed full of periods. Every line has at least one. In other
poems the reader has to figure out all the phrasing for herself—
where the pauses and grammatical groupings have to occur.

One fellow poet, whose advice I respect, felt I should make all the poems in the manuscript adhere to that latter principle. Wrestling with that advice, that possibility, helped me realize and then refine what I was doing with my fluctuating use of periods and commas in the book.

The character (who eventually, over the years of working on the book, ceased to be me) was finding new ways to perceive and shape reality, but only after a sort of dissolving feeling, a falling apart. I'm pretty sure most people who have gone through a divorce (with or without children, with or without the legal contract) know what I'm talking about. Your recovery is dependent upon being able to handle the resulting period of being *at sea*, and then an ability to start putting things back together, but in new ways, in new patterns. I like to think the coming-and-going of the punctuation and other rules mirrors that process.

I also found a tremendous lightness in working without those rules, in using white space and line breaks instead of caps or punctuation. A surprising new language evolved, and, like the surprise of being single again, turned out to expand rather than ruin the world. It could be gimmicky, and as poets we have to beware that danger, but if used in a muscular way, as a technique that pushes the language to greater precision and force, I think it makes a superb exercise for any poet. Anyway, I hope I pulled it off.

DL: The strictness of the 3-line stanzas seems at odds with the abandonment of punctuation and capitalization. Tell us why that disparity.

NW: I love the regular look of repeating stanza sizes, but I hate received rhythms and almost never work in received forms. Jazz is more my kind of music. I love spondees that throw the whole train of a poem off the tracks. There's no better fun than shifting the rhythm of a line—and yet I hate set rhythm. Maybe it's cheating, but I still like to build in the contradiction of a set stanza size, so the poem has a formal look to it even if there is no received form at work. I used a lot of couplets and tercets (all unrhymed) in my book, *Detour,* 2-line stanzas because the book is about the letting go of a two-person relationship, 3-line stanzas to show a more stable form, where a third possibility keeps growing out of jarring pairs. I hope I achieved some kind of useful paradox in appearing formal but being in fact pretty loose when it came to standard rules. I want to say this paradox reflects the institution of marriage itself. There's a formal pact, about which we make an enormous deal with lots of ceremony and so on, but the proof is in the daily pudding, not the formal or legal arrangement.

DL: Another structural device here is the catalog of both the beloved's body parts and his personal attributes. The selection of items and the order in which they appear—random or calculated?

NW: At first such things are fairly random, but as you revise, you start moving things around. I definitely wanted a mixture of the concrete and the abstract, the parts and the attributes. When you fall in love, you are responding to such an organic mix of parts: the body, the movements, the feelings projected, a million tiny cues about personality and attitude and history. The poem contains by no means an exhaustive list, but I did want it to give a sense of the smorgasbord of elements in a person that I was, long ago, responding to.

DL: You speak of *his appearance golden,* but end with *his darkness is love.* Please explain the apparent contradiction.

NW: You know how first there's the person of the poet writing out of experience and probably some primitive desire to express an emotion or a thought or *the self* or whatever it is. And then as poets we have to refine what happens and ask ourselves brutally whether that spurt can ever really become a poem that's worth anyone else reading. It could take a couple of years of revising for me to know; I'm pretty slow. The *him* who got this poem started was indeed quite beautiful, and he did have a golden quality. Handsome, smart, and people looked up to him. The darkness came over time. It's the darkness of a person who couldn't rise to the occasions of later life, and who breaks things in his effort to avoid growing up, or facing the music, or whatever it is that a midlife crisis demands of us. By the end of our relationship, or of the development of the poem, his love really was no more than darkness, had been snuffed out. The line used to read *his darkness his love*, as if they were two separate and possibly battling things. But in the end I decided they had become one entity, and that it was a *love* I did not want to partake of.

DL: I was both amused and surprised by *his lack of hangnails*. Why do you praise the beloved for not having something so insignificant? Would it be a strike against him if he did have hangnails?

NW: I admired his lack of hangnails at first, for the plain reason that I always had them—from worry, from habit. So I envied the smooth hands. As the poem developed, though, and I started adding and taking out details, I realized that his lack of worry was part of his *darkness*. How one person can remain serene, even if only on the polished surface, while recklessly disemboweling a family, a love, is really a cause for horror and not for admiration. So the non-hangnails took on quite a different meaning, but also became emblematic for me of how my own understanding of the situation changed over time. What had seemed beautiful was, under the surface, the opposite. Isn't remorse our saving grace? So some hangnails would have been nice. Also, though, as a writer I just like to mix up the types of detail that I'm using, just to keep my own mind and the reader's mind hopping. Predictability, too much pattern, isn't what I'm looking for in poetry—my own or other people's.

Bonus Prompt: The Egomaniacal Cento

A cento is technically a poem made entirely of lines cut from other poems, poems by other poets.

But let's vary that. Instead of borrowing lines from other poets, use your own lines, the ones you've discarded from your own poems, the ones sitting in a journal, the best lines from failed poems.

You might make a project of this one day by going through all your old folders and culling lines. While doing this, don't even be thinking about the poem you might create. Just gather and gather. Feel free to add in a snippet of overheard conversation or something you heard on TV.

Then on another day, go through the list and circle or mark lines that seem to go together. Pull them out and put them together.

Rearrange if you like, adjust the diction, make additions where they feel needed. You can do whatever you like. These are, after all, your words to do with as you please.

Suggested Reading

Allende, Isabel. *Aphrodite: A Memoir of the Senses*. Harper Perennial, 1999.

Bayles, David, and Ted Orland. *Art and Fear: Observations on the Perils (and Rewards) of Artmaking*. Image Continuum Press, 2001.

Birnbaum, Molly. *Season to Taste: How I Lost My Sense of Smell and Found My Way*. Ecco, 2011.

Brown, James, and Diana Raab, eds. *Writers on the Edge: 22 Writers Speak about Addiction and Dependency*. Modern History Press, 2012.

Cameron, Julia. *The Artist's Way: A Spiritual Path to Higher Creativity*. Tarcher, 2002.

Cohen, Sage. *Writing the Life Poetic: An Invitation to Read and Write Poetry*. Writer's Digest Books, 2009.

Dobyns, Stephen. *Best Words, Best Order*. 2nd edition. Palgrave MacMillan, 2003.

Doty, Mark. *The Art of Description: World into Word*. Graywolf Press, 2010.

Fish, Stanley. *How to Write a Sentence: And How to Read One*. Harper, 2011.

Fogel, Alice B. *Strange Terrain: A Poetry Handbook for the Reluctant Reader*. Hobblebush Books, 2009.

Grimm, Susan, ed. *Ordering the Storm: How to Put Together a Book of Poems*. CSU Poetry Center, 2006.

Hoagland, Tony. *Real Sofistikashun: Essays on Poetry and Craft*. Graywolf Press, 2006.

Hughes, Holly J., and Brenda Miller. *The Pen and the Bell: Mindful Writing in a Busy World*. Skinner House Books, 2012.

Hugo, Richard. *The Triggering Town: Lectures and Essays on Poetry and Writing*. Reissue edition. W. W. Norton, 2010.

Hunley, Tom C. *The Poetry Gymnasium: 94 Proven Exercises to Shape Your Best Verse*. McFarland, 2011.

Kowit, Steve. *In the Palm of Your Hand: The Poet's Portable Workshop*. Tilbury House, 1995.

McNair, Wesley. *Mapping the Heart: Reflections on Place and Poetry*. Carnegie Mellon, 2003.

McNair, Wesley. *The Words I Chose: A Memoir of Family and Poetry*. Carnegie Mellon, 2012.

Mercer, Jeremy. *Time Was Soft There: A Paris Sojourn at Shakespeare and Co.*, Picador, 2006.

Minar, Scott, ed. *The Working Poet: 75 Writing Exercises and a Poetry Anthology*. Autumn House Press, 2009.

Neubauer, Alexander, ed. *Poetry in Person: Twenty-five Years of Conversations with America's Poets*. Knopf, 2010.

Raab, Diana, ed. *Writers and Their Notebooks*. University of South Carolina Press, 2010.

Skinner, Jeffrey. *The 6.5 Practices of Moderately Successful Poets: A Self-Help Memoir*. Sarabande Press, 2012.

Skloot, Floyd. *The Wink of the Zenith: The Shaping of a Writer's Life*. Bison Books, 2011.

Tharp, Twyla. *The Creative Habit: Learn It and Use It for Life*. Simon & Schuster, 2003.

Wiggerman, Scott, and David Meischen, eds. *Wingbeats: Exercises and Practice in Poetry*. Dos Gatos Press, 2011.

Winterson, Jeanette. *Why Be Happy When You Could Be Normal?* Grove Press, 2012.

Contributors

Kim Addonizio is the author of five poetry collections, most recently *Lucifer at the Starlite* (W. W. Norton, 2011), a finalist for the Poets Prize and the Northern California Book Award. She is also the author of *Ordinary Genius: A Guide for the Poet Within* (W. W. Norton, 2009). Her honors include a Guggenheim Fellowship, two National Endowment of the Arts Fellowships, and Pushcart Prizes for both poetry and the essay.

JoAnn Balingit was appointed Delaware's Poet Laureate in 2008. She is the author of *Your Heart and How It Works* and *Forage*, which won the 2011 Whitebird Chapbook Prize from Wings Press. Her poems have appeared in such journals as *Smartish Pace, PoetsArtists*, and *Salt Hill Journal*, as well as on *Verse Daily*. She teaches poetry in schools and non-profits and works with the Delaware Division of the Arts.

Ellen Bass is the author of two full-length poetry books. *The Human Line* (Copper Canyon) was named a Notable Book of 2007 by the *San Francisco Chronicle*. Her first collection, *Mules of Love* (BOA Editions, 2002), won the Lambda Literary Award. Other awards include the New Letters Poetry Prize, a Pushcart Prize, and a Fellowship from the California Arts Council. She teaches in the low-residency MFA program at Pacific University.

Jan Beatty is the author of four poetry books. Her newest is *The Switching/Yard* (University of Pittsburgh, 2013). Her poetry has appeared in journals such as *Gulf Coast, Indiana Review*, and *Court Green*. Her awards include the 1994 Agnes Lynch Starrett Prize, the Pablo Neruda Prize for Poetry, and two fellowships from the Pennsylvania Council on the Arts. She is director of the creative writing program at Carlow University

Jeanne Marie Beaumont is the author of three collections of poetry, most recently *Burning of the Three Fires* (BOA Editions, 2010). She co-edited the anthology *The Poets' Grimm: Twentieth Century Poems from Grimm Fairy Tales* (Story Line Press, 2003). She teaches at The Unterberg Poetry Center of the 92nd Street Y in Manhattan and in the Stonecoast MFA Program at the University of Southern Maine.

Robert Bense's book of poems, *Readings in Ordinary Time*, was published in 2007 by The Backwaters Press. His poems have appeared in *Poetry, Salmagundi, Agni*, and *The New Republic*, among many other magazines.

Pam Bernard is the author of three poetry collections, including *Blood Garden: An Elegy for Raymond* (Turning Point, 2010). She has received fellowships from the National Endowment of the Arts, the Massachusetts Cultural Council, and the MacDowell Colony. Her poems have appeared in *TriQuarterly, Spoon River Poetry Review, Prairie Schooner*, and elsewhere.

Michelle Bitting's second book, *Notes to the Beloved*, won the 2011 Sacramento Poetry Center Award. Her earlier collection, *Good Friday Kiss*, won C&R Press's DeNovo First Book Award. Her work has appeared in *American Poetry Review, Prairie Schooner, Nimrod*, and elsewhere. Her poems have also been featured on *Poetry Daily* and *Verse Daily*.

Deborah Bogen's third collection, *Let Me Open You a Swan*, won the 2009 Antivenom Prize from Elixir Press. Her first full-length collection, *Landscape with Silos*, won the 2005 X. J. Kennedy Poetry Prize (Texas Review Press). Her poems and reviews have appeared in *Shenandoah, The Gettysburg Review, The Georgia Review*, and elsewhere. Her work has also been featured on *Poetry Daily* and *Verse Daily*.

Kathryn Stripling Byer served from 2005-2009 as North Carolina's first woman Poet Laureate. She is the author of six books of poetry, most recently *Descent*. Her awards include the Hanes Poetry Award, the Southern Independent Booksellers Alliance Poetry Award, and the Roanoke-Chowan Award. Her work has appeared in such journals as *The Georgia Review, Shenandoah*, and *Southern Poetry Review*.

Edward Byrne is the author of six books of poetry, most recently *Tinted Distances* (Turning Point, 2011). His poems have appeared in journals such as *American Poetry Review, Missouri Review*, and *North American Review*. He is the editor of *Valparaiso Poetry Review* and an English professor at Valparaiso University.

Kelly Cherry was Poet Laureate of the Commonwealth of Virginia, 2010-2012. She is the author of twenty books of fiction, poetry, memoir, essay, and criticism. Her collection, *Hazard and Prospect*

(Louisiana State University, 2007), was a finalist for the Poets' Award. She was the first recipient of the Hanes Poetry Prize for a body of work and was the 2012 recipient of the Carole Weinstein Poetry Prize.

Philip F. Deaver is the author of *How Men Pray* (Anhinga Press, 2005). His poems have been published in *The Florida Review, Measure,* and *Poetry Miscellany,* as well as read by Garrison Keillor on *The Writer's Almanac.* He is writer-in-residence and Professor of English at Rollins College and teaches in the brief residency MFA program at Spalding University.

Bruce Dethlefsen was Poet Laureate of Wisconsin, 2011-2012. He is the author of two chapbooks and two full-length collections, most recently *Unexpected Shiny Things* (Cowfeather Press, 2011). A retired library director, he now devotes his time to writing and supporting poetry. He also plays in a band, "Obvious Dog," that performs at poetry readings. His work has been read by Garrison Keillor for *The Writer's Almanac.*

Caitlin Doyle has taught at Penn State University as the Emerging Writer Resident in Creative Writing. Her honors include an Amy Award, an Artist Grant through the Elizabeth George Foundation, and residency fellowships at the MacDowell Colony and the Ucross Foundation. Her poetry has appeared in *The Atlantic, The Boston Review, Best New Poets 2009,* and elsewhere.

Patricia Fargnoli was the New Hampshire Poet Laureate from 2006-2009. Her third book, *Then, Something* (Tupelo Press, 2009), won the Foreword Magazine Silver Book Award and was co-winner of the Sheila Mooton Book Award. *Duties of the Spirit* (Tupelo Press, 2005) won the Jane Kenyon Literary Award. *Necessary Light* (Utah State University Press, 1999) won the May Swenson Book Award. She has published poems in such journals as *Harvard Review, Ploughshares,* and *Green Mountains Review.*

Ann Fisher-Wirth is the author of four full-length poetry books, including *Dream Cabinet* (Wings Press, 2012). She is coeditor of *The Ecopoetry Anthology* (Trinity University Press, 2013). Her awards include the Rita Dove Poetry Award, a Poetry Award from the Mississippi Institute of Arts and Letters, and two Poetry Fellowships from the Mississippi Arts Commission. She teaches at the University of Mississippi.

Amy Gerstler is the author of seven books of poetry, most recently *Dearest Creature* (Penguin, 2009). Her book *Bitter Angel* (1990) won the National Book Critics Circle Award. Her work has also appeared in *The New Yorker, Paris Review, American Poetry Review*, and elsewhere. She is a core faculty member at the Bennington Writing Seminars, Bennington College, Vermont.

Karin Gottshall is the author of *Crocus* (Fordham University Press, 2007) and two chapbooks. Her work has appeared in such journals as *The Gettysburg Review, Field*, and *The Virginia Quarterly Review*. She teaches poetry writing at Middlebury College.

Jennifer Gresham is the author of *Diary of a Cell*, which won the 2004 Steel Toe Books Poetry Prize. Her work has appeared in such journals as *Prairie Schooner, Alaska Quarterly Review*, and *Rattle*. Several of her poems have also been featured by Garrison Keillor on *The Writer's Almanac*.

Bruce Guernsey is Distinguished Professor Emeritus at Eastern Illinois University where he taught for twenty-five years. His work has appeared in such journals as *Poetry, Southern Review*, and *Willow Springs*, and has been featured on Ted Kooser's *American Life in Poetry*. A former editor of *Spoon River Poetry Review*, he has published four collections of poetry, including *From Rain: Poems, 1970-2010* (Ecco Qua Press).

Marilyn Hacker is the author of twelve books of poems, most recently *Names* (W. W. Norton, 2010). She is the recipient of the 2009 American PEN Award for Poetry in Translation, the Lenore Marshall Award, the Poets' Prize, the National Book Award, two Lambda Literary Awards, and the PEN Voelcker Award in Poetry. A Chancellor of the Academy of American Poets, she lives in New York and Paris.

Jeffrey Harrison is the author of five full-length books of poetry, most recently *What Comes Next*, which won the 2011 Dorset Prize competition from Tupelo Press. His fourth book, *Incomplete Knowledge* (Four Way Books), was runner-up for the 2008 Poets' Prize. A recipient of Guggenheim and National Endowment of the Arts Fellowships, he has published his work in *The Yale Review, American Poetry Review, The Hudson Review*, and elsewhere.

Lola Haskins is the author of *The Grace to Leave* (Anhinga, 2012), her tenth collection. Her ninth, *Still, the Mountain*, won the Silver

Medal for Poetry in the 2010 Florida Book Awards. She is also the author of *Not Feathers Yet: A Beginner's Guide to the Poetic Life* (Backwaters, 2007). She teaches in Pacific Lutheran University's low-residency MFA program.

Jane Hirshfield is the author of seven poetry collections, most recently *Come, Thief* (Knopf, 2011). Her awards include fellowships from the Guggenheim and Rockefeller Foundations, the National Endowment for the Arts, and the Academy of American Poets. In 2012 she was elected a chancellor of the Academy of American Poets, and also named the third recipient of the Donald Hall-Jane Kenyon Award in American Poetry.

Gray Jacobik is the author of six poetry books. Her latest, *Little Boy Blue: A Memoir in Verse*, is from CavanKerry Press. She is a recipient of a National Endowment of the Arts Fellowship and a Connecticut Artist's Fellowship and has been awarded the Yeats Prize, the X. J. Kennedy Poetry Prize, and the AWP Poetry Series Award. Her poems have appeared in *The Kenyon Review, Poetry, The Georgia Review*, and elsewhere.

Rod Jellema is the author of *Incarnality: The Collected Poems* (Wm. B. Eerdmans, 2010) and four other books of poems. He was twice awarded poetry writing fellowships by the National Endowment for the Arts and was many times a resident fellow at Yaddo. He is Professor Emeritus at the University of Maryland, where he was the founding director of the Creative Writing Program.

Richard Jones is the author of seven books of poetry, including *The Correct Spelling & Exact Meaning* (Copper Canyon, 2010). *The Blessing: New and Selected Poems* received the Midland Authors Award for Poetry for 2000. He is editor of the literary journal *Poetry East* and is currently professor of English at DePaul University in Chicago.

Julie Kane was appointed Louisiana's Poet Laureate in 2011. She is the author of three full-length poetry collections. *Jazz Funeral* won the 2009 Donald Justice Poetry Award. Honors for her poetry include a Fulbright Scholarship, an Academy of American Poets Prize, the George Bennett Fellowship in Writing at Phillips Exeter Academy, and a Glenna Luschei Prairie Schooner Poetry Award.

Adele Kenny is the author of five full-length poetry collections, including *What Matters* which received the 2012 International Book

Award for poetry. She is the recipient of two poetry fellowships from the New Jersey State Council on the Arts, a Merton Poetry of the Sacred Award, and an Allen Ginsberg Poetry Award. She is poetry editor of *Tiferet Journal* and director of the Carriage House Poetry Series.

Dorianne Laux is the author of five books of poetry, most recently *The Book of Men* (W. W. Norton, 2011). She is also co-author of *The Poet's Companion: A Guide to the Pleasures of Writing Poetry*. Her awards include a Pushcart Prize, two fellowships from the National Endowment for the Arts, and a Guggenheim Fellowship. She teaches poetry at North Carolina State University and is founding faculty at Pacific University's low- residency MFA Program.

Sydney Lea was appointed Poet Laureate of Vermont in 2011. He has published ten volumes of poetry, including *Young of the Year* (Four Way Books, 2011). He has also published a novel, two collections of naturalist essays, and *A Hundred Himalayas: Essays on Life and Literature* (University of Michigan, 2012). He founded the *New England Review* in 1977 and edited it until 1989. He is the recipient of fellowships from the MacArthur, Rockefeller, and Fulbright Foundations.

Hailey Leithauser's debut poetry collection, *Swoop* (Graywolf Press, 2013), won the 2012 Emily Dickinson First Book Award from the Poetry Foundation. Her work has been featured on *Poetry Daily* and published in *Best American Poetry 2010* and in such journals as *The Gettysburg Review, Pleiades*, and *Poetry*.

Jeffrey Levine is the author of two books of poetry, most recently *Rumor of Cortez* (Red Hen Press, 2005). His first book, *Mortal, Everlasting*, won the 2002 Transcontinental Poetry Prize. His other prizes include the James Hearst Poetry Prize, the Mississippi Review Poetry Prize, and the 2007 American Literary Review Poetry Prize. He is the founder, editor-in-chief, and publisher of Tupelo Press.

Denise Low served as Poet Laureate of Kansas from 2007-2009. Her ten books of poetry include *Ghost Stories of the New West* (Woodley Press, 2010). She is a member of the national board of the Associated Writers & Writing Programs and served as its president 2011-12. She has awards from the Lannan Foundation, Academy of American Poets, and Kansas Arts Commission.

Jennifer Maier's collection, *Dark Alphabet*, won the Crab Orchard Review Series in Poetry First Book Award. Her poetry has appeared in numerous journals, including *Poetry, American Poet*, and *Mississippi Review*. Her work has also been featured on *Poetry Daily* and *The Writer's Almanac*. She teaches at Seattle Pacific University and serves as Associate Editor of the journal *Image*.

Marie-Elizabeth Mali is the author of *Steady, My Gaze* (Tebot Bach, 2011) and co-editor of the anthology, *Villanelles* (Everyman's Library Pocket Poets, 2012). Her work has appeared in *Calyx, Poet Lore, Rattle*, and elsewhere. She served as co-curator for the LouderARTS Reading Series from May 2008 through December 2011.

Jeffrey McDaniel is the author of five books of poetry, most recently *Chapel of Inadvertent Joy* (University of Pittsburgh Press, 2013). His poems have been published in many anthologies and magazines, including *Best American Poetry 2010, Ploughshares*, and *American Poetry Review*. A recipient of a fellowship from the National Endowment for the Arts, he is a professor of creative writing at Sarah Lawrence.

Wesley McNair was appointed Poet Laureate of Maine in 2011. He has authored nine collections of poetry, including *Lovers of the Lost: New and Selected Poems* (Godine, 2010). He has also written several non-fiction books, including *The Words I Chose: A Memoir of Family and Poetry* (CMU, 2012). He has received grants from the Fulbright and Guggenheim Foundations, two Rockefeller Fellowships, and two National Endowment for the Arts Fellowships.

Susan Laughter Meyers is the author of *My Dear, Dear Stagger Grass*, winner of the inaugural Cider Press Review Editor's Prize. Her first book, *Keep and Give Away*, won the South Carolina Poetry Book Prize. She is the recipient of the 2013 Carrie McCray Nickens Poetry Fellowship as well as fellowships from the Virginia Center for the Creative Arts and the South Carolina Academy of Authors.

Bronwen Butter Newcott has published poems in *Indiana Review, Prairie Schooner, Missouri Review*, and other journals. She received her MFA from the University of Maryland, spent several years in Southern California where she taught high school English, then returned to Washington DC.

Alicia Ostriker has published twelve books of poetry, including *The Book of Seventy* and *The Book of Life: Selected Jewish Poems 1979-*

255

2011. Among her critical works are *Writing Like a Woman* and *Stealing the Language: The Emergence of Women's Poetry in America*. Retired from Rutgers University, she now teaches in the MFA program at Drew University.

Linda Pastan served as Poet Laureate of Maryland from 1991 to 1995. She has published thirteen books of poetry, most recently *Traveling Light*. She has twice been a finalist for The National Book Award and in 2003 won the Ruth Lilly Prize for Lifetime Achievement. She was on the staff of the Breadloaf Writers Conference for twenty years.

Stanley Plumly was named in 2009 as the Poet Laureate of Maryland. *Orphan Hours* (W. W. Norton, 2012) is the most recent of his ten collections of poetry. His honors include a Rockefeller Foundation Fellowship, Ingram-Merrill Fellowship, Guggenheim Fellowship, three National Endowment for the Arts Fellowships, and eight Pushcart Prizes.

Vern Rutsala is the author of numerous poetry collections, most recently *Other Voices: Translations & Variations* (Trask House, 2011). *The Moment's Equation* was a finalist for the 2004 National Book Award. He has received a Guggenheim Fellowship, two National Endowment for the Arts Fellowships, two Carolyn Kizer Poetry Prizes, a Pushcart Prize, and the Richard Snyder Prize.

Martha Silano's third book, *The Little Office of the Immaculate Conception*, won the 2010 Saturnalia Books Poetry Prize. She is the recipient of fellowships from Seattle 4Culture and the Washington State Artist Trust. Her work has appeared in *Agni, American Poetry Review, Beloit Poetry Journal*, and elsewhere. She teaches composition and creative writing at Bellevue College.

Marilyn L. Taylor, former Poet Laureate of the state of Wisconsin, is the author of six collections of poetry. Her poems have appeared in many anthologies and journals, including *Poetry, The American Scholar*, and *Able Muse*, as well as in Ted Kooser's *American Life in Poetry*. She taught creative writing for fifteen years at the University of Wisconsin-Milwaukee and was a contributing editor for *The Writer* magazine.

Matthew Thorburn is the author of three books of poems, most recently *This Time Tomorrow* (Waywiser Press, 2013). He is the recipient of a Witter Bynner Fellowship, the Mississippi Review Prize, and two Dorothy Sargent Rosenberg Poetry Prizes. His poems have appeared in such journals as *The Paris Review, Poetry*, and *Prairie Schooner*.

Lee Upton is the author of five books of poetry and the author of a book of creative nonfiction, *Swallowing the Sea: On Writing & Ambition, Boredom, Purity, & Secrecy* (Tupelo Press, 2012). Her awards include the Lyric Poetry Award, a Pushcart Prize, the National Poetry Series Award, and the Miami University Novella Award. She is the Writer-in-Residence and a professor of English at Lafayette College.

Nance Van Winckel is the author of *Pacific Walkers*, her sixth collection of poems (University of Washington Press, 2013). She is the recipient of two National Endowment of the Arts Fellowships, a Pushcart Prize, and awards from the Poetry Society of America, *Poetry*, and *Prairie Schooner*. Her poems have appeared in many journals, including *The Southern Review, Field*, and *The Gettysburg Review*. She teaches in the MFA in Writing Program at Vermont College of Fine Arts.

Ingrid Wendt is the author of six full-length books of poems, most recently *Evensong* (Truman State University Press, 2011). She is also the author of one chapbook, two anthologies, a book-length teaching guide, and numerous articles and reviews. A Poetry Consultant with the National Council of Teachers of English, she has received the Oregon Book Award, the Carolyn Kizer Award, an Oregon Literary Arts Fellowship, and the D. H. Lawrence Award.

Nancy White is the author of two books: *Sun, Moon, Salt*, winner of the Washington Prize, and *Detour* (Tamarack Editions, 2010). Her poems have appeared in *Black Warrior Review, Ploughshares, Virginia Quarterly Review*, and elsewhere. She teaches at Adirondack Community College in upstate New York, is an associate editor at *The Sow's Ear Poetry Review*, and serves as editor and president of The Word Works.

Cecilia Woloch is the author of five collections of poetry, most recently *Carpathia* (BOA Editions, 2009). Her chapbook, *Narcissus*, won the Tupelo Press 2006 Snowbound Series Award. She teaches in the creative writing program at the University of Southern California and is the founding director of The Paris Poetry Workshop. She is a recipient of a 2011 National Endowment of the Arts Fellowship.

Baron Wormser is the author of two books on craft, a book of short stories, a memoir, and nine books of poetry. A former school librarian, he created the Conference for Poetry and Teaching at The Frost Place in New Hampshire. The Poet Laureate of Maine from 2000-2005, he now lives in Vermont and teaches in the low-residency MFA program at Fairfield University.

Suzanne Zweizig's poetry has appeared in such publications as *32 Poems, Beloit Poetry Journal, Subtropics*, and *Poet Lore*, and has been featured on *Verse Daily*. She was a semi-finalist for The Nation/Discovery prize in 2003 and has received fellowships from the MacDowell Colony, the Virginia Center for the Creative Arts, and the Washington DC Arts Commission.

Credits

About the Author

Diane Lockward is the author of three poetry books, most recently *Temptation by Water*. Her previous books are *What Feeds Us*, which received the 2006 Quentin R. Howard Poetry Prize, and *Eve's Red Dress*. She is also the author of two chapbooks, *Against Perfection* and *Greatest Hits: 1997-2010*. Her poems have been published in a number of anthologies, including *Poetry Daily: 360 Poems from the World's Most Popular Poetry Website* and Garrison Keillor's *Good Poems for Hard Times*. Her poems have also appeared in such journals as *Harvard Review, Spoon River Poetry Review*, and *Prairie Schooner*, and have been featured on *Poetry Daily, Verse Daily*, and *The Writer's Almanac*. She is the recipient of a Poetry Fellowship from the New Jersey State Council on the Arts and awards from *Best of the Net, North American Review, Louisiana Literature, Journal of New Jersey Poets*, and *Naugatuck River Review*. She is a former high school English teacher and Poet-in-the-Schools for the New Jersey State Council on the Arts.

NOTES —

CPSIA information can be obtained at www.ICGtesting.com
Printed in the USA
LVOW13s1606180614

390646LV00003B/558/P